officeinteriors

Conception: Arian Mostaedi

Publishers: Carles Broto & Josep Mª Minguet

Editorial Coordination: Jacobo Krauel

Architectural Adviser: Pilar Chueca

Graphic Design & Production: Héctor Navarro

Text: Contributed by the architects,
edited by Jacobo Krauel and Jennifer Brown

Cover photograph: © Tim Soar

© Carles Broto i Comerma (All languages, except Spanish)
Ausias Marc 20, 4-2. 08010 Barcelona, Spain
Tel.: +34 933 012 199 Fax: +34 933 026 797
www.linksbooks.net · info@linksbooks.net

ISBN: 84-89861-51-X
D.L.: B- 7165-2003
Printed in Barcelona, Spain

officeinteriors

index

introduction

The work environment, as a space for professional and interpersonal exchange, has undergone dramatic changes in recent years. The continuing swift pace of developments in communication technology, with a new, more timeless, ubiquitous and portable handling of information, has greatly contributed to these changes. Gone are the bulky file cabinets and expansive tables of yesteryear, with work surfaces having been reduced to the size of a computer. Tele-work and videoconferencing are further indications of this omnipresence.

At the same time, however, is an ever-increasing trend towards sustainability in architecture, as evidenced by energy-saving measures, alternative energy sources and the use of new materials.

These, and a host of additional concerns particular to office design, greet the architect and interior designers when drawing up the plans for a new workspace. The company's corporate identity, for example, must be somehow translated into the volumes of the interior spaces, as well as of the building as a whole. The modern office also requires versatility and dynamism – it must be flexible enough to quickly adapt to a range of uses. It must be aesthetically pleasing, and should encourage interpersonal communication amongst employees, while significantly lessening outdated hierarchical barriers. Such is the case in the program designed by Carlos Manzano, with its city-like structure, complete with avenues, a central square and a port. Lorcan O'Herlihy and Pugh+Scarpa, on the other hand, favor open, diaphanous spaces, where the environment is neither visually nor hierarchically divided. To accomplish this same end, Klein Dytham's design has opted for horseshoe shaped workstations which can accommodate up to 85 people a day, thereby eliminating private offices.

In Hemmi-Fayet's program, color as a central aspect in spatial design is closely related to the company's work in, among other activities, computer simulated flight.

Another original program is the highly atypical design from the Design Blue studio. Here, we find an illuminated space in which a series of oversized pedestal-chairs predominate, providing a sensation of openness, in spite of the minimal amount of allotted space.

In short, this is a concise, yet wide-ranging, volume, bringing together examples of renovated spaces as well as entirely new ground plans – proposals which comprise an invaluable source of inspiration and a concentrated study of the challenges involved in creating new workspaces.

Tham Videgård Hansson in collaboration with Snowcrash
Snowcrash Office and showroom
Stockholm, Sweden

Tham Videgård Hansson Architects were commissioned to remodel an old industrial building in Stockholm for Snowcrash, a Swedish-Finnish company that develops concepts and products for work and home.

The building offered a full 28x42x3 m pillar deck floor with light from the east, west and south. Apart from the open office and showroom, the brief also included a workshop, a prototype atelier, and an apartment for visiting designers.

The new office layout combines an effective open office with defined rooms of varying size. The aim was to create an optimum work environment, and aspects such as acoustics, lighting and air were studied. The main design element is a continuous, free formed, glass wall inserted into the existing warehouse structure. The undulating glass core creates defined places within the premises: showroom, east office, kitchen, west office. Simultaneously it constitutes a link in between all areas, both visually and logistically.

Since no doors have been placed in the glass facing the open office, the amount of accessible free wall surface is increased and the risk of disturbance between the meeting room and the office is minimized. As a result, a visual and spatial pause is created (as a buffer) in the transition from work to meeting. Deep grey in the passageways underlines this spatial contrast. The color scheme is otherwise atelier-like; with light, neutral tones.

Photographs: Åke E: Son Lindman

Floor plan

1. Entrance
2. Showroom
3. Reception
4. Copy room
5. Storage furniture
6. Phone booth
7. Storage
8. Prototype atelier
9. Workshop
10. Project & meeting room

11. Office - Design development
12. Office - Administration
13. Canteen
14. Meeting room
15. Office & art meeting room
16. Sitting room
17. Pantry
18. Guestroom
19. Computer room
20. Cloud

With the initial idea of creating a contemporary environment that communicates the Snowcrash state of mind, the architects opted for open and fluid solutions rather than a closed and final form. Designed as one continuous space, the architecture enhances the impression of a company where everyone works together, 'interweaving' professional skills.

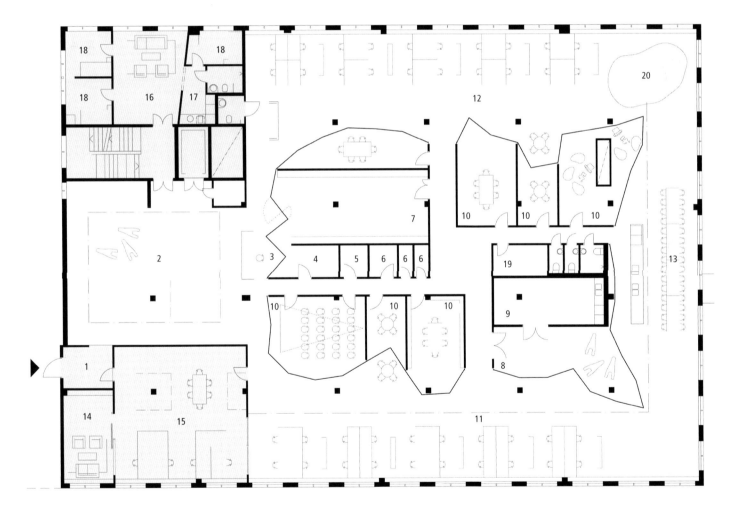

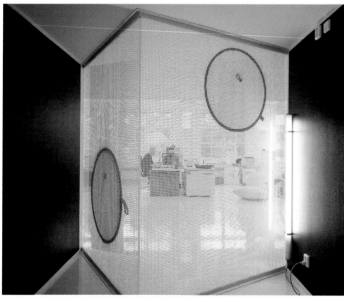

The staff canteen and the entrance, pictured opposite, are floored in glossy epoxy. Both the kitchen counter in the canteen and the reception desk in the entrance are covered in green athletic rubber flooring. Sculptural Chip lounges by Teppo Asikainen and Ilkka Terho grace the reception area.

The walls of the War Room, with the irregular glass partitions, are clad in blackboard for mapping out strategies and ideas.

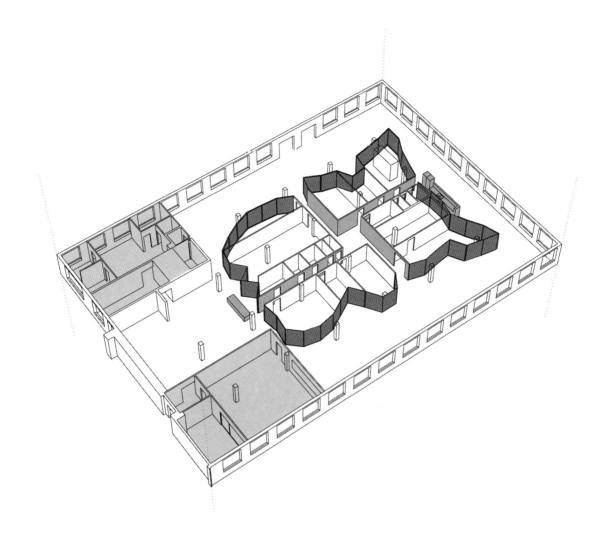

Marmol Radziner and Associates
TBWA \ Chiat \ Day Offices
San Francisco, USA

Marmol Radziner and Associates received the commission to renovate an 85-year-old four-story warehouse near the San Francisco Bay for the advertising firm of TBWA \ Chiat \ Day. The architects sought inspiration for the design in the site's maritime history, and the architectural forms and materials are a reference to the ships buried beneath the building as well as the cargo crates stored in the former warehouse.

By stripping the building down to its existing brick walls, wood ceilings, timber columns and large glass windows, the space and access to natural light are significantly improved.

A huge, upwardly curving wall of rough horizontal boards, recalling a fragment of a wooden ship's outer hull, draws visitors through the lobby. The upper floor has been cut away to reveal other curving laminated forms, which suggest the ribs of oddly configured ships. Only partially visible overhead, these elements form the structure of translucent polycarbonate-lined conference and project rooms on the second level.

In special areas, such as a lounge, the floor is covered in cork, while elsewhere floor cladding is sealed, construction-grade plywood. The two floors of office space follow mostly an open plan, where custom-built plywood stations stand in neat orthogonal rows.

Photographs: Benny Chan / Fotoworks

Section

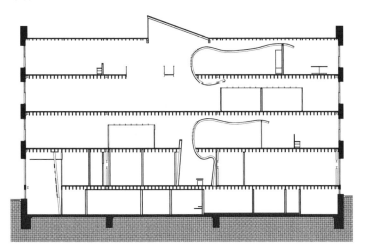
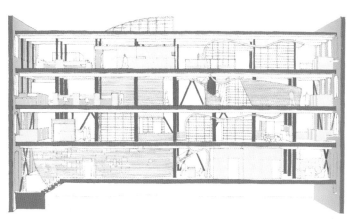

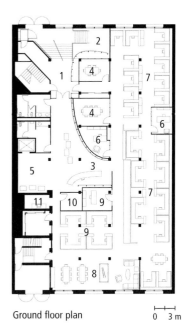

1. Entrance
2. Void
3. Reception
4. Meeting
5. Elevator lobby
6. Office
7. Workstations
8. Play area
9. Production
10. Viewing
11. Kitchen

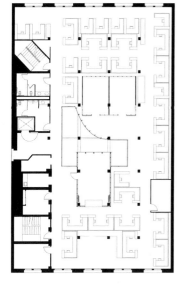

Ground floor plan

0　3 m

First floor plan

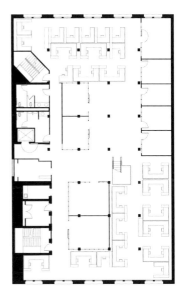

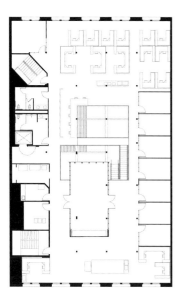

Second floor plan   Third floor plan

Foster and Partners
The Design Centre
Essen, Germany

This former powerhouse in an Essen coal-mining complex forms part of an extraordinary group of early 20th century buildings, all with red-brown painted exposed steel I-beams, and an infill of industrial glazing and red brick. These magnificent structures, with their towering chimneys and vast halls, are the cathedrals of the industrial age. The powerhouse has an inner hall of colossal proportions, as impressive as any Gothic edifice. The challenge was to adapt this building to create a new home for the German Design Centre, without fundamentally altering its character.

The building's façade was restored and a number of later additions were removed to reveal its original form. Inside, the heavy industrial feel of the building has been conserved. One of the large boilers was preserved intact as an example of 1930's technology. The remaining four boilers were removed and replaced by independently supported galleries, which are articulated from the existing structure as 'boxes within a box', their lightness juxtaposed with the heaviness of the original fabric. A simple concrete cube contains further exhibition space as well as conference rooms with views of the surrounding complex and the landscape. Visitors enter via the dramatic central hall where the rusty steel structure and exposed brick walls are still visible.

Together with associated offices, the Design Centre houses a combination of temporary and permanent exhibitions – everything from cars to electrical appliances – that are constantly updated and require highly flexible galleries. The different exhibition areas and the interaction of old and new architecture, create a varied backdrop for the location of exhibits, while the changing nature of the exhibitions themselves adds a further dynamic element to this relationship.

Photographs: Nigel Young / Foster and Partners

Ground floor plan

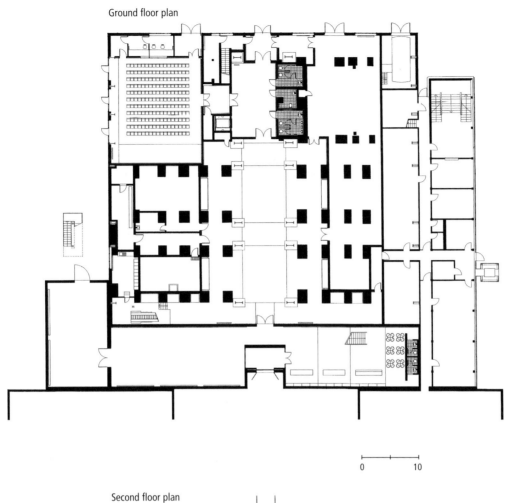

0   10

Second floor plan

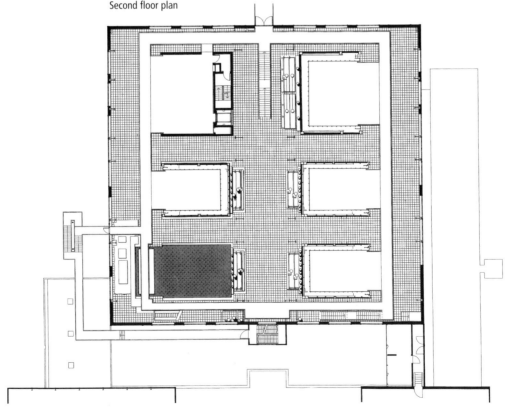

The final project in this powerhouse conserves the original red-brown painted exposed steel I-beams, and an infill of industrial glazing and red brick. Highly flexible galleries have been provided for a combination of temporary and permanent exhibitions that are constantly updated.

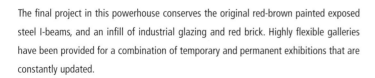

Fourth floor plan

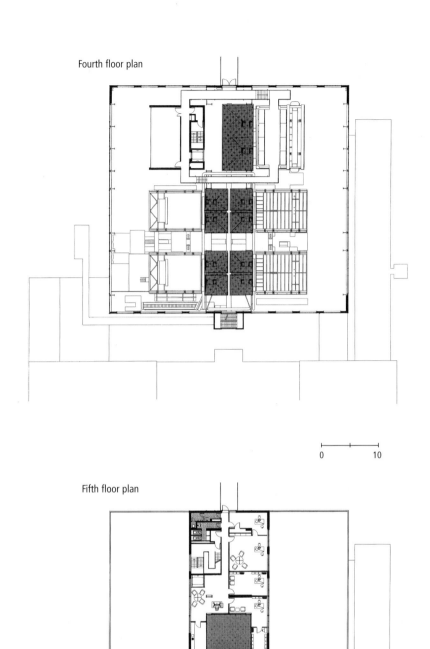

0   10

Fifth floor plan

Longitudinal section

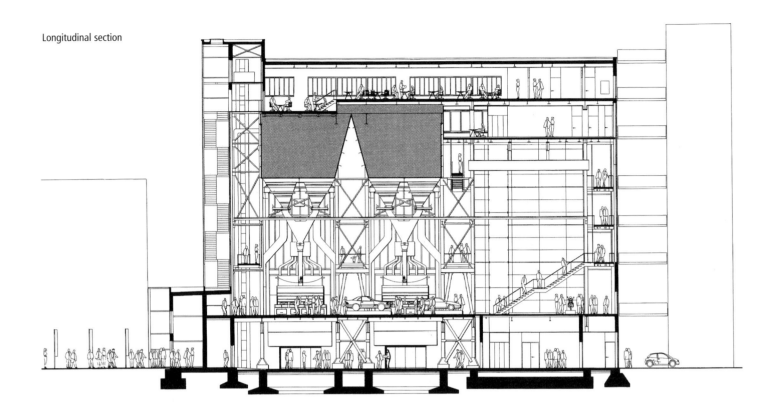

The heavy industrial feel of the building has been conserved by leaving much of the listed structure exposed and un-restored. Four of the five boilers were gutted and two floors of galleries inserted. They provide a blank canvas for the exhibitions whilst still revealing the upper parts of the boilers. These galleries are accessed from the outer edges and are linked to each other by a walkway with glass balustrades.

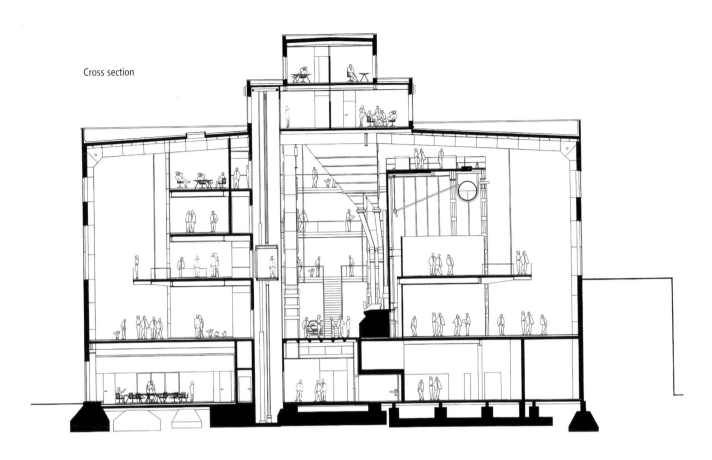

Cross section

Klein Dytham architecture
Beacon Communications office
Tokyo, Japan

The newly formed advertising agency, Beacon Communications, wanted to move into offices that reflected their unique approach to advertising and allowed for a different working style. Located in a new 17-floor office tower, the four-story, 56,300 ft^2 office interior features wild curves, Day-Glo colors and very open offices.

Each of the column-free floors is divided into open workspace traversed by an undulant 15 ft wide 'ribbon', within which shared functions are lined up like train compartments. The lowest floor houses reception, management, and support areas, while the other levels are devoted to ad development. For individual workstations, the designers arranged an office system in horseshoe clusters that can accommodate up to 85 workers per day.

Company directors have not only foregone private offices but also desks. Each director has a chair of his or her choice, a filing cabinet on wheels and a spot at a collective directors' work area. Clad in white plastic laminate, this station has an inviting openness. The ribbon's meeting rooms are accessible from either side, each of the four ribbons has a sheet frame covered with plasterboard, rising to become the ceiling over a conference room, stepping down to form screening-area seating, or swooping low to provide a platform for a test kitchen. Beacon decided upon floor themes to divide the agency; Woman, Man, Family and Community. Materials and colors revolve around the themed floors with the ribbon on the male floor in steel, wood on the family floor and a pink snakeskin pattern on the female floor.

Photographs: Kozo Takayama

Section

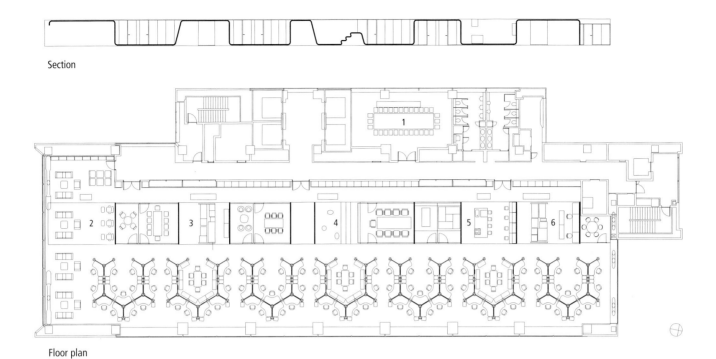

Floor plan

Section

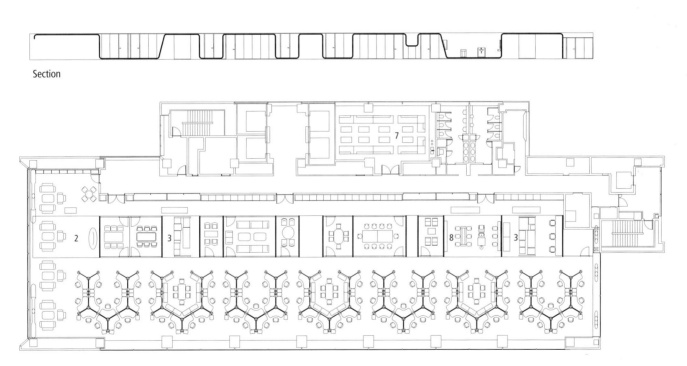

Floor plan

1. New business workshop
2. Library
3. Printer center
4. Chat Space
5. Kitchen
6. Painter center

7. Agency forum
8. Make up space
9. Pub
10. Print production
11. Studio

Although there are no enclosed private offices, everyone is a few steps from the ribbon, where there are small offices for private conversations or quiet meetings. To facilitate communication between management and staff, the directors work around a 12 m long dining table with the company president. The idea is that anyone within the company can pull up one of the 20 dining chairs around the table and have a chat. For the corporate boardroom, clear glazing can be turned filmy when greater privacy is required.

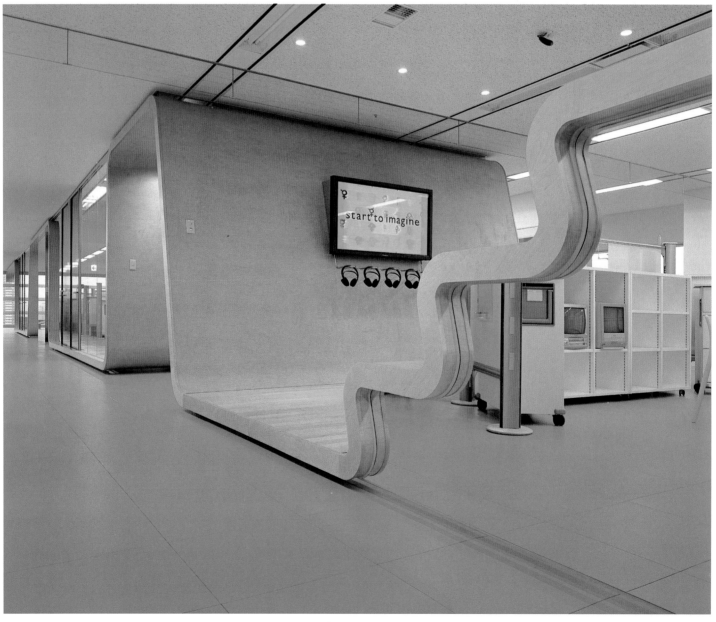

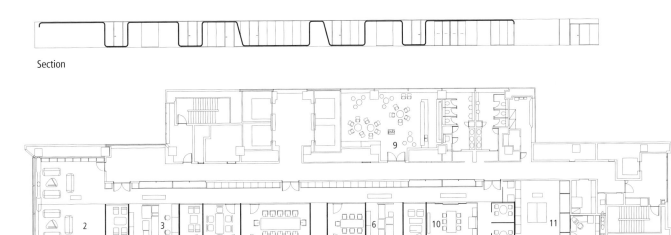

Section

Floor plan

2. Library
3. Printer center
6. Painter center
9. Pub
10. Print production
11. Studio

Construction detail

1. White polyvinyl chloride sheet; ribbon edge baked painted steel (white).
2. Mirror
3. Bed space: special ordered polyvinyl tile (pink snake skin); ribbon R-part steel plate+decorated wall cloth
4. Kitchen corian top counter (white); drawer, side panel: white UV paint; skirting: stainless steel hair line finish
5. Floor: maple wood flooring; edge: maple wood veneer

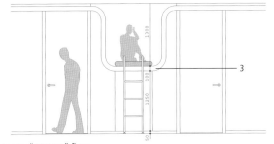

Chat space: "Community" floor

Capsule space: "Woman" floor

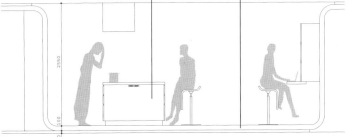

Kitchen: "Family" floor

Kauffmann Theilig & Partner
Freie Architekten BDA
Werdich Headquarter Offices
Dornstadt, Germany

Built in the 1970's and guided by functional and economical criteria, Werdich's central offices consisted of a ground floor building and a separate warehouse, built with prefabricated sections of reinforced concrete. Company growth forced the office surface to be extended about 2,000 m², giving the buildings their own identity.

The extension consisted of a new three-story block between the office building and the existing warehouse: a curved, wooden shell inclined upwards with large glass panels. The external part of the building's shell represents a visible company feature, as well as being the main entrance to the building. It is formed by aluminum tubes that act as parasols and filter the view of the adjacent blacktop roofs.

In the lower part, a large communicative space connects the different levels of offices. Among other services, this building accommodates meeting rooms and small staff cafeterias, an elevator and glazed staircases.

The rectangular openings in the shell have been optimized from the technical point of view of lighting, providing daily light to the three levels of offices and balconies.

As regards the location, the site is on Lerchenbergstrasse, with sweeping views to the south. The other views are limited by very heterogeneous industrial buildings and by the state highway. The construction available forced the projection of an architectural body facing longitudinally from east to west, with the offices facing north and south, towards the jumbled flat roofs of the adjacent industrial buildings.

Photographs: Roland Halbe /Artur

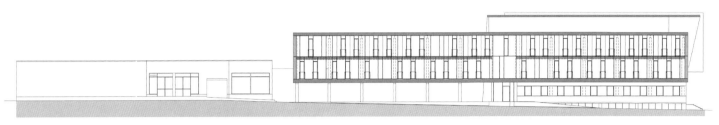

East elevation

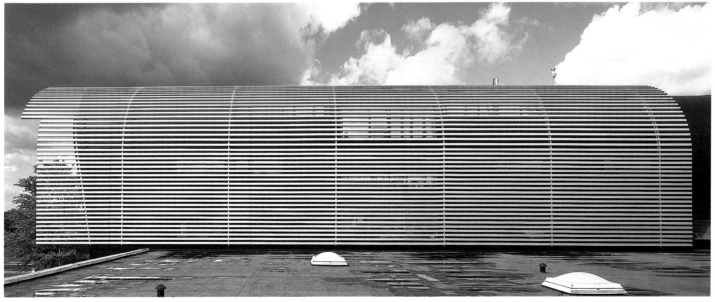

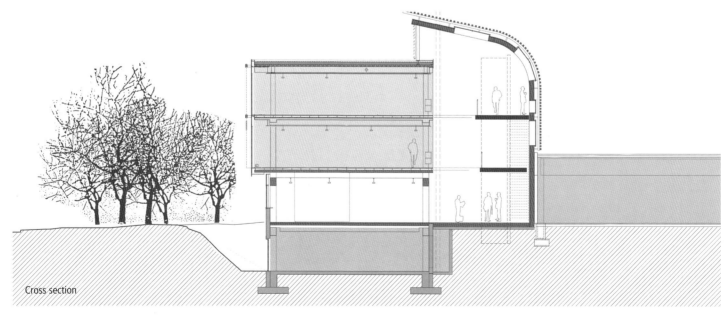

Cross section

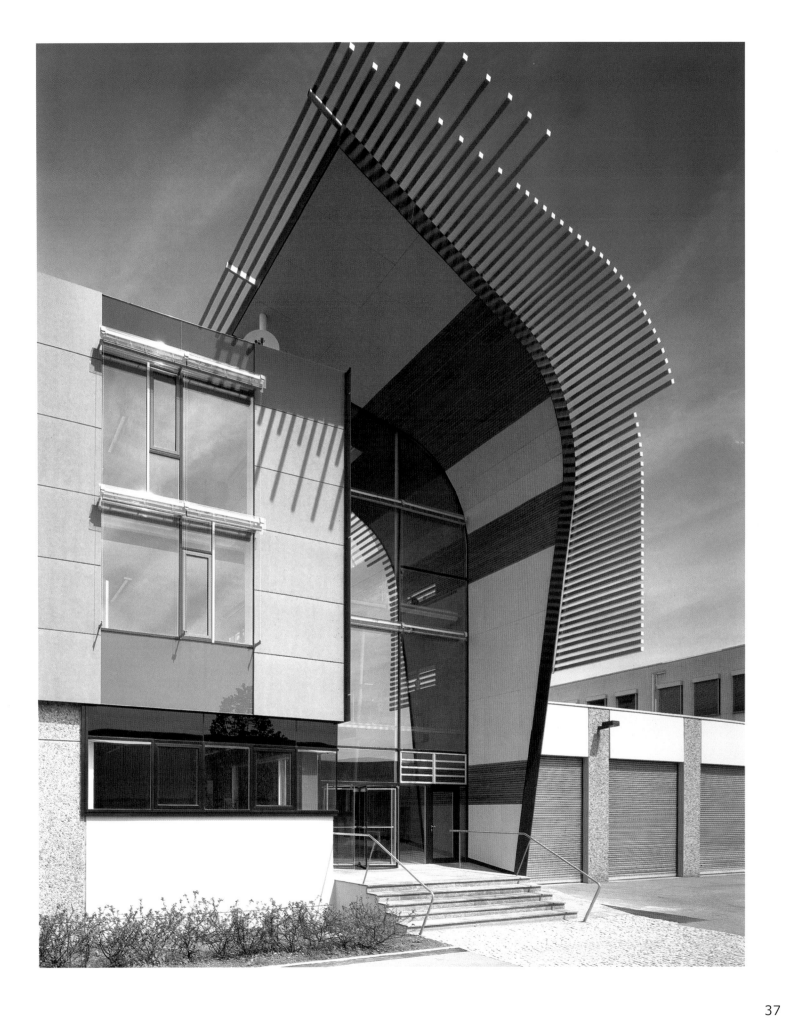

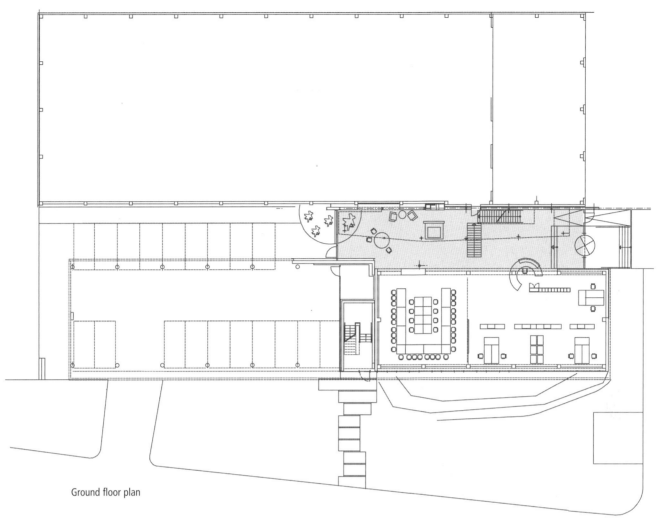

Ground floor plan

Depending on their use, the different floors can be converted into space for individual offices, for groups or as a large open-plan space. The versatile and full-length glazed separating walls act as an acoustic barrier as well as offering the necessary transparency. All this generates an open and communicative office space, completely focussed on satisfying user requirements.

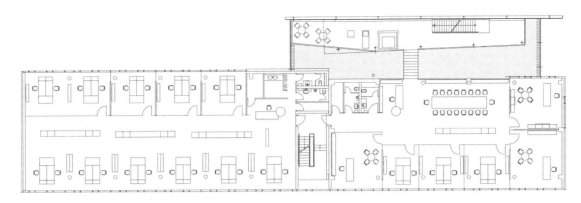

First floor plan

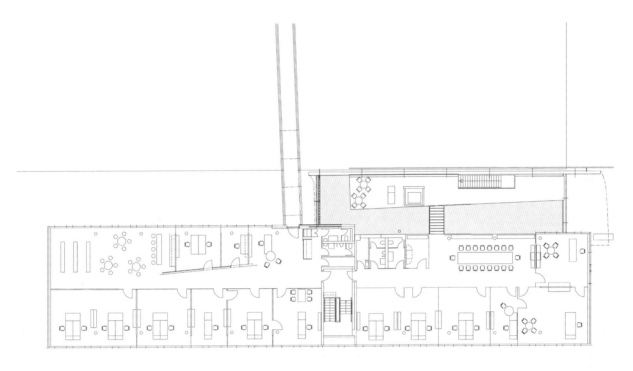

Second floor plan

Denys & Von Arend + Guy Sonet
Renault Design Barcelona
Barcelona, Spain

The aim of this commission was to create a favorable environment where the company's design team could carry out its creative work, while conserving the industrial feel of the building.

The solution proposed has been a combination of pure lines, clear spaces and soft colors with bare brick walls, double heights, exposed installations, and metal and glass enclosures.

One of the key resources has been the treatment of light and color. The lighting of each space is designed to subtly magnify the contrast between the elegant shapes, simple brickwork and steel enclosures. The color blue recurs repeatedly and is lit up and reflected in ceilings and glass faces, introducing a discordant note into the general harmony.

Another of the important elements of the project has been the creation of warm, comfortable, almost homelike spaces that are more reminiscent of a home workshop than an office.

The entrance works as a multi-purpose open space, presided over by the library, and with a rest area furnished like a living room.

Using the existing pillars, the ground floor is divided into two spaces by a row of large cupboard-blocks that separate the work area (on the façade side) from the reception and presentation area (on the courtyard side). Finally, the meeting room and executive office are closed off by a glass screen, in front of which has been placed an iron screen.

Photographs: Joan Mundó

Floor plan

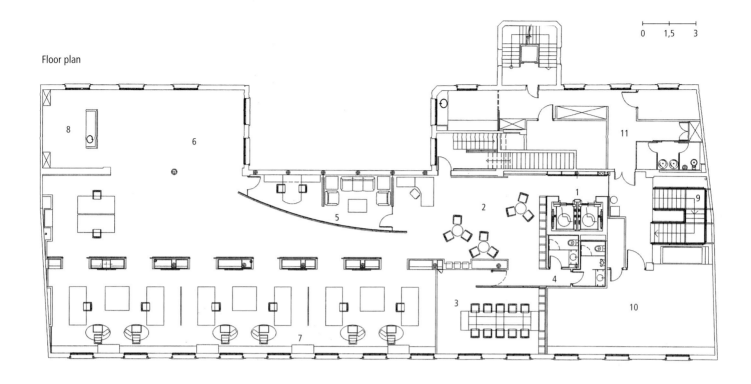

1. Hall
2. Reception-Library
3. Meeting room
4. Bathroom
5. Manager's office
6. Presentation room
7. Design room
8. Storage
9. Stairway
10. Layout workshop
11. General services

Interior courtyard

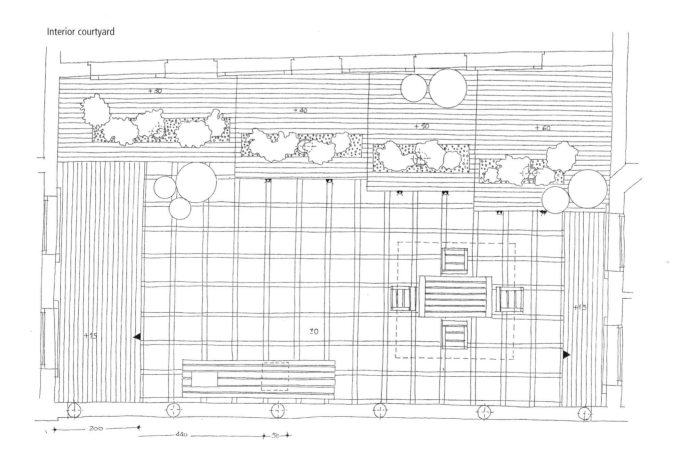

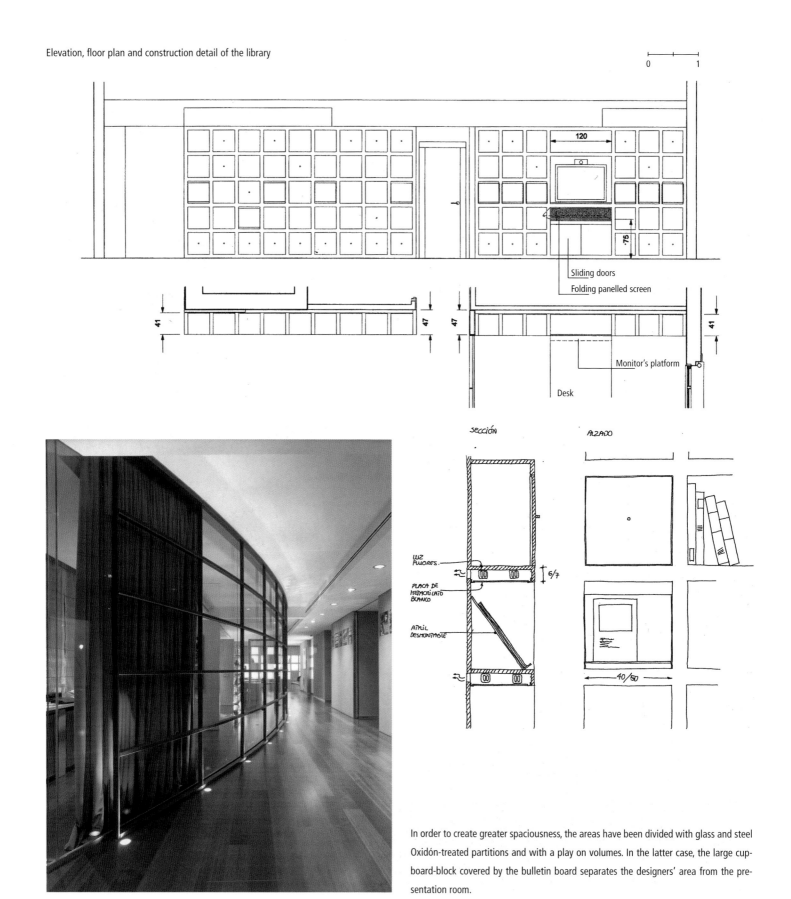

0   1

120

·75

Sliding doors

Folding panelled screen

41   47   47   41

Monitor's platform

Desk

SECCIÓN   ALZADO

LUZ
FLUORES.

PLACA DE
METACRILATO
BLANCO

ATRIL
DESMONTABLE

6/7

40/50

In order to create greater spaciousness, the areas have been divided with glass and steel Oxidón-treated partitions and with a play on volumes. In the latter case, the large cupboard-block covered by the bulletin board separates the designers' area from the presentation room.

Construction detail of reception desk

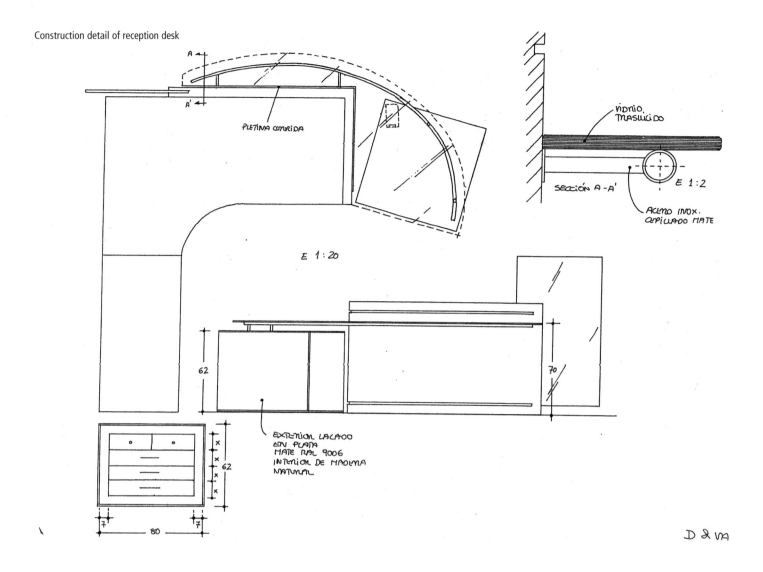

PLETINA CORRIDA

E 1:20

VIDRIO.
TRASLUCIDO

SECCIÓN A - A'   E 1:2

ACERO INOX.
CEPILLADO MATE

62

70

EXTERIOR LACADO
EN PLATA
MATE RAL 9006
INTERIOR DE MADERA
NATURAL

62

7   80   7

D 2 VA

Construction detail
of management desk

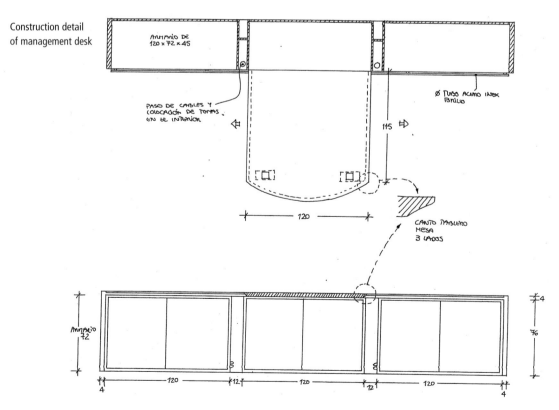

ARMARIO DE
120 x 72 x 45

PASO DE CABLES Y
COLOCACIÓN DE TOMAS
EN EL INTERIOR

Ø TUBO ACERO INOX
BRILLO

115

120

CANTO MADERO
MESA
3 LADOS

ARMARIO
72

76

4

120   12   120   12   120

4   4

Construction detail of
video conference room

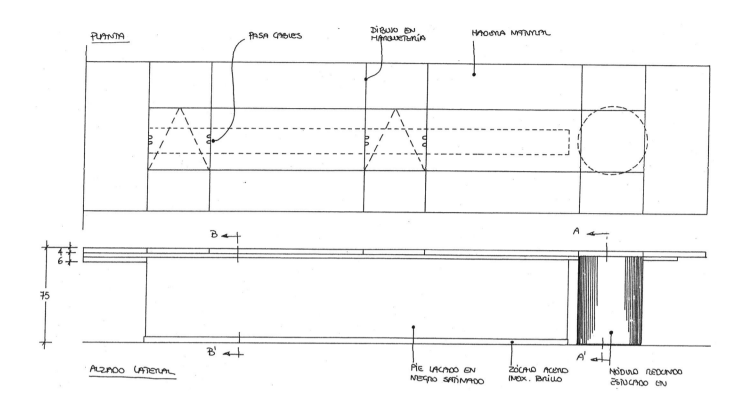

PLANTA

PASA CABLES

DIBUJO EN
MARQUETERÍA

MADERA NATURAL

B

A

4
6

75

B'

ALZADO LATERAL

PIE LACADO EN
NEGRO SATINADO

ZÓCALO ACERO
INOX. BRILLO

A'

MÓDULO REDONDO
ESILUCADO EN

Construction detail
of Rimón table

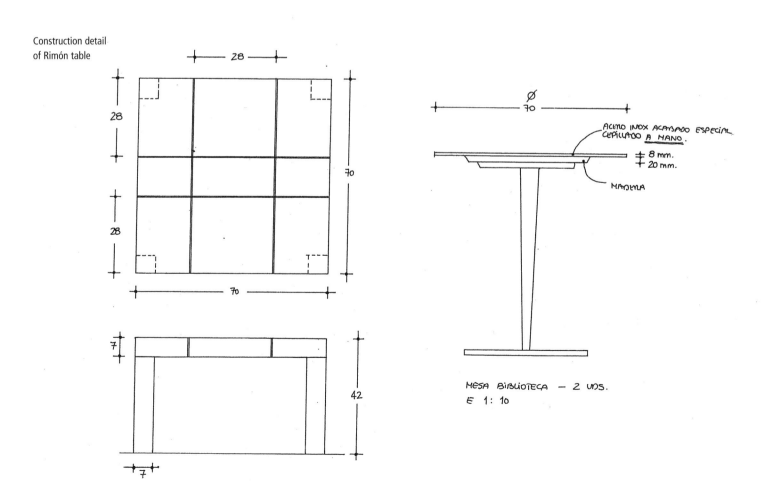

28

28

28

70

70

7

42

7

∅
70

ACERO INOX ACABADO ESPECIAL
CEPILLADO A MANO.

8 mm.
20 mm.

MADERA

MESA BIBLIOTECA — 2 UDS.
E 1: 10

51

The service elevator, located next to the stairs, is enclosed in a sand-treated glass box and illuminated in blue. This latter resource recurs repeatedly in ceilings and glass faces with the idea of introducing a discordant note into the general harmony.

The Segurit glass used in the bathrooms is acid etched with fillets, and lets light through while maintaining privacy.

Bathroom section

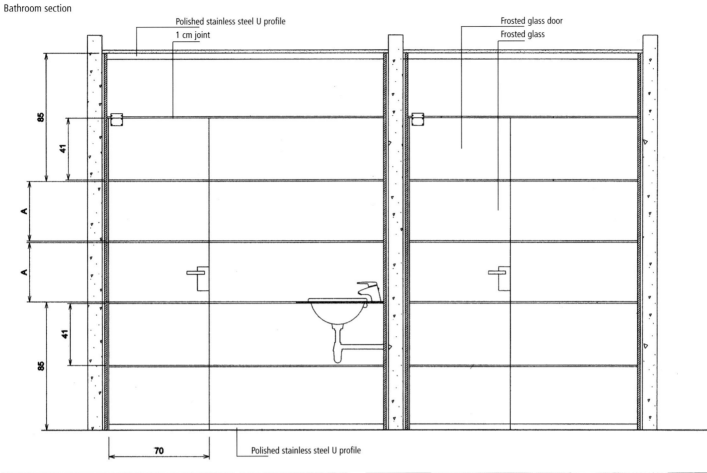

Polished stainless steel U profile
1 cm joint

Frosted glass door
Frosted glass

85
41
A
A
41
85

70

Polished stainless steel U profile

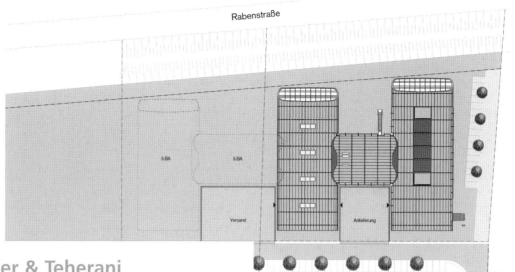

Bothe, Richter & Teherani
Company Building Tobias Grau
Rellingen, Germany

The goal was to create a sophisticated architecure with means as simple as possible, such as timber glue truss beams. The original task consisted of the new erection of a commercial building for the company Tobias Grau with 30 employees at the time. The floor plan covers a prefab parts warehouse with areas for final assembly, delivery and shipping, as well as an office section for the commercial and design departments.

Now, with the completion of the second building phase, the building has been extended with a plan meant to respond to new demands of design, work flow and cost.

The first building phase consists of an elongated, oval edifice. A second, identical shape has been executed as the extension and connected to the first building by a two-story, almost square edifice.

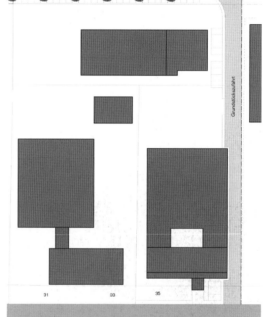

The construction consists of timber glue truss beams spanning over 20 m, which were erected at a distance of 5 m and which support the external aluminum skin made of Alucobond plates. An inserted concrete table in the first building results in two-story use and at the same time serves as reinforcement. This concrete table is formed as a soffit in cross cap shape with a hog of 10 cm and stands on filigree concrete supports. On the upper floor the structure is completed by wooden rocking piers.

The building was executed completely free of support columns, as a large hall with timber glue truss beams was constructed accordingly.

As a result of the company's involvement in the lighting sector the opportunity arose for the company Tobias Grau —as owner of the building— to develop all lights anew, for this building in particular, and then for mass production. Areas which feature new lighting elements include the conference room, the toilets, stairwell, cafeteria and work stations.

The architecture of this company's building will thus partially function as an impulse for ideas and as a trigger for product and program development.

Photographs: Michael Wurzbach

Site plan

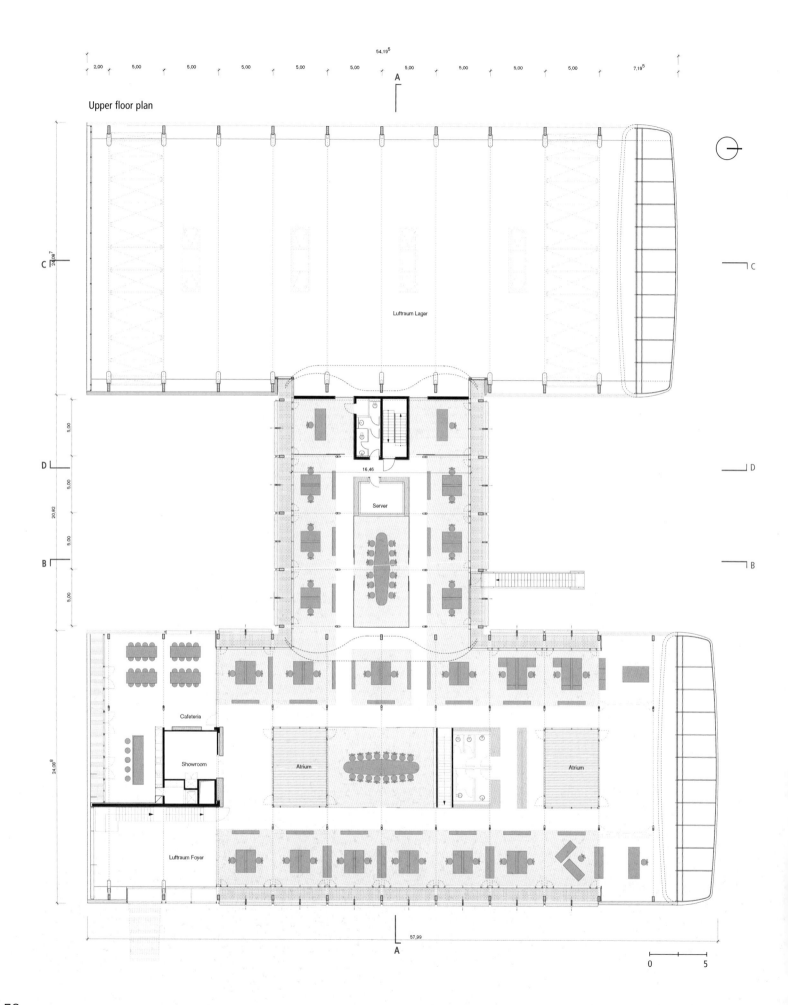

Upper floor plan

54,19⁵

2,00 5,00 5,00 5,00 5,00 5,00 5,00 5,00 5,00 5,00 7,19⁵

A

C

Luftraum Lager

D

16,46

Server

B

Cafeteria

Showroom

Atrium

Atrium

Luftraum Foyer

57,99

A

0   5

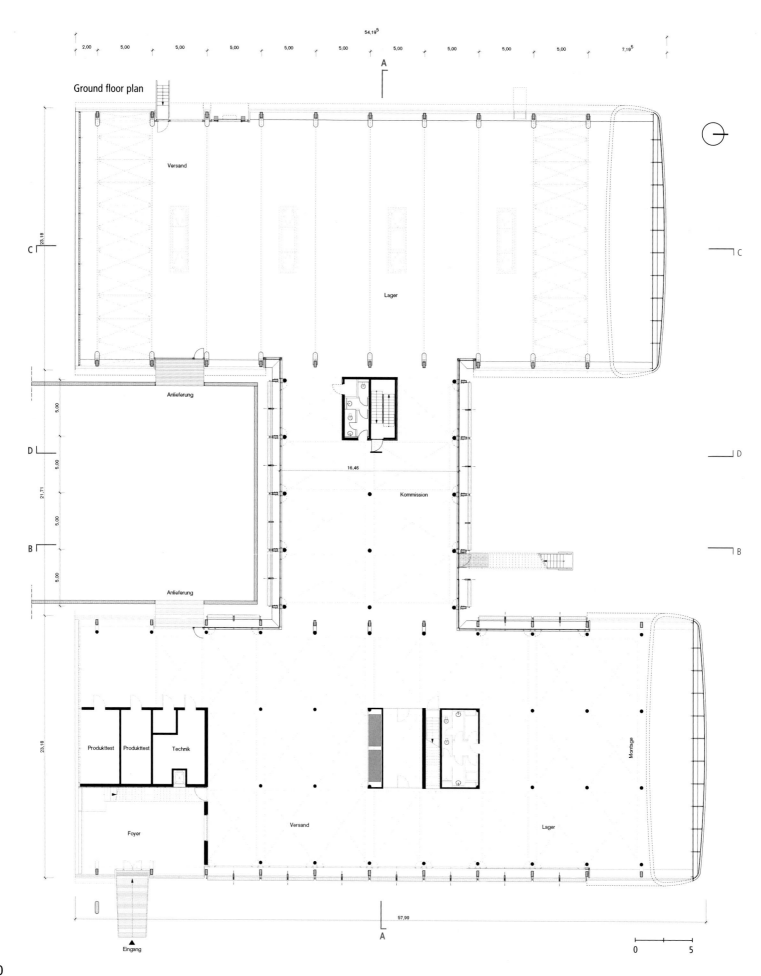

Ground floor plan

54,19⁵

2,00   5,00   5,00   5,00   5,00   5,00   5,00   5,00   5,00   5,00   5,00   7,19⁵

A

C   23,18

Versand

Lager

C

Anlieferung

5,00

D   5,00

16,46

D

21,71

Kommission

5,00

B   5,00

B

Anlieferung

Montage

23,18

Produkttest   Produkttest   Technik

Foyer

Versand

Lager

A   57,99   A

Eingang

0   5

The building consists of timber glue truss beams spanning over 20 m, which were erected at a distance of 5 m, and which support the external aluminum covering, made of Alucobond sheets. An inserted cross-shaped concrete table in the first building results in two-story use and at the same time serves as reinforcement.

North elevation

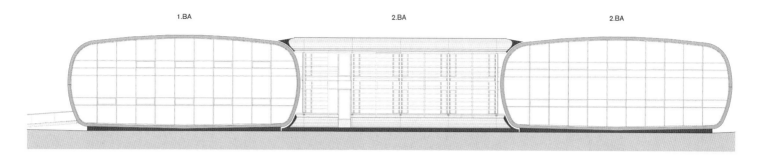

1.BA   2.BA   2.BA

South elevation

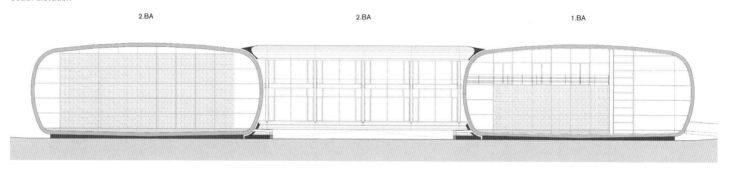

2.BA   2.BA   1.BA

West elevation

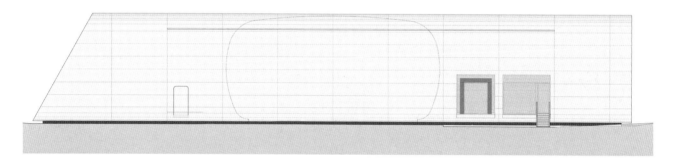

Section AA

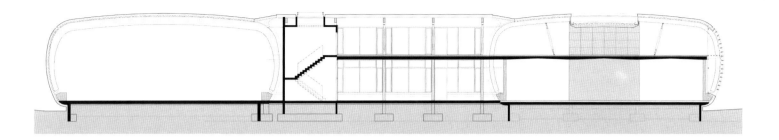

Section BB

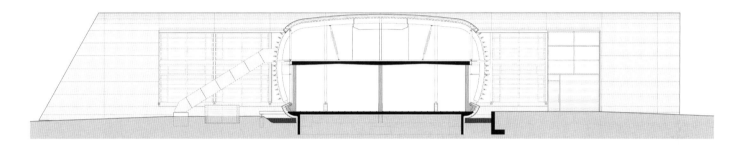

Section CC

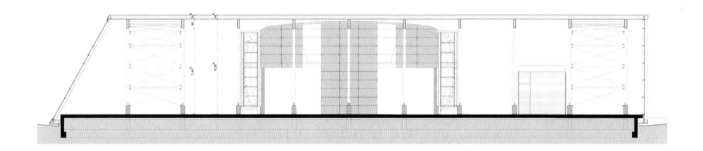

Section DD

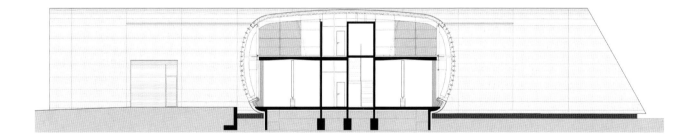

63

The building was executed completely free of support columns, as a large hall with timber glue truss beams was constructed accordingly. On the upper floor, the structure is completed by wooden rocking piers. As a result of the company's involvement in the lighting sector, all lights in this project were developed anew.

Richard Hywel Evans
Architecture & Design Ltd]
Cellular Operations Headquarters
Swindon, UK   www.rhe.uk.com

Cellular Operation's call center in Swindon has been celebrated in the national Press and Television as 'the happiest work place in Britain'. One of the company's objectives when commissioning the building to Richard Hywel Evans was to create an excellent working environment and a striking corporate identity. Another consideration was to design a flexible office space, paramount in a call center environment.

The end result was 4500 m² of column-free space in a building that combines high technology with international-style serenity.

The main structure of the building is a mass concrete frame which stores heat in winter and is cool in summer. Large sections of the south-facing façade are glazed in Okalux insulated glass, allowing daylight to penetrate with little solar gain.

Service and plant rooms are located on the second floor, behind an elegantly louvered 'tower', looking out across the main two-story work-space. Behind the service area, which also houses the Perspex lifts, are the main conference rooms and offices. These break out of the traditional rectilinear partitions in favor of an organic approach that reflects the building's exterior.

However, it is the great bulbous glass extension, supported on slim steel tubular columns, that is the highlight of the building. The spectacular curved façade brings daylight deep into the building and functions as the key element in a simple ventilation system, drawing cool air off the adjoining lake, which is then dispersed through a network of vents running through the floor to the south area of the building.

Photographs: John N. MacLean & Tim Soar

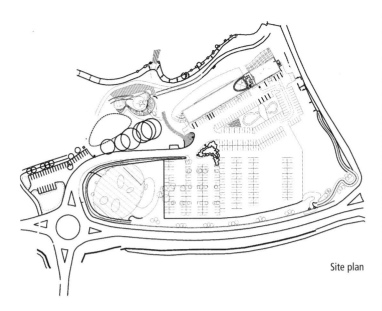

Site plan

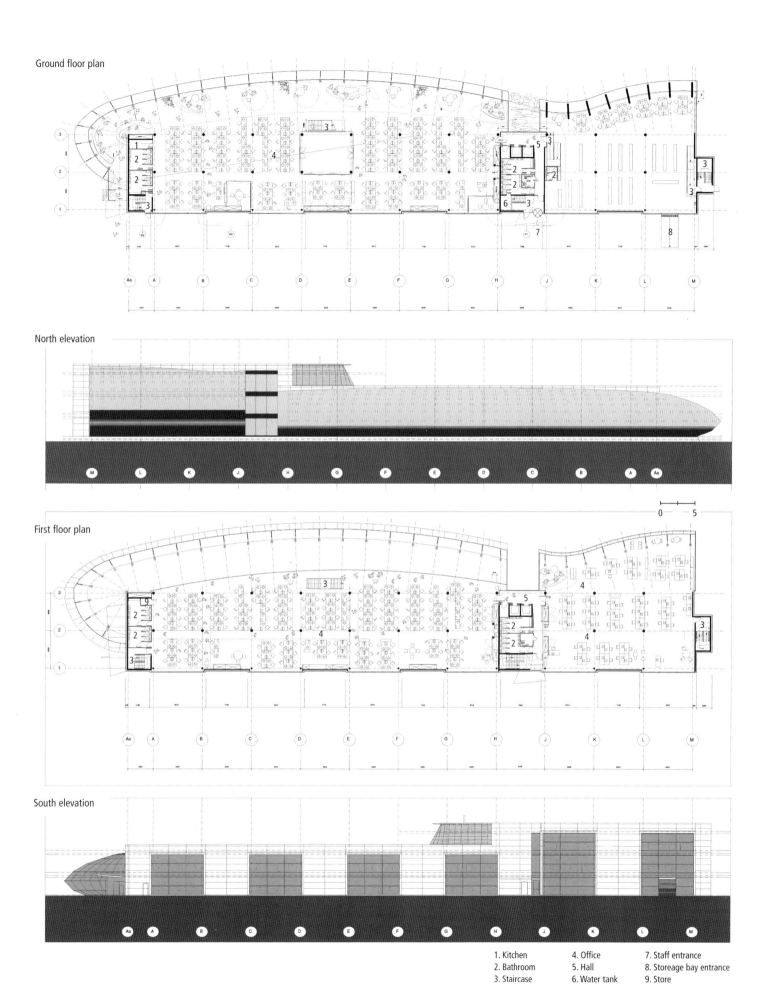

Ground floor plan

North elevation

First floor plan

South elevation

1. Kitchen
2. Bathroom
3. Staircase
4. Office
5. Hall
6. Water tank
7. Staff entrance
8. Storeage bay entrance
9. Store

69

Second floor plan

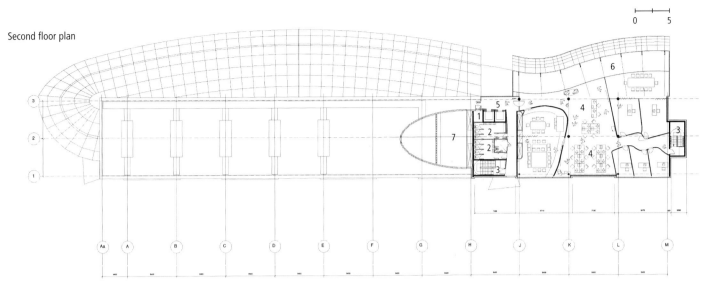

East elevation   West elevation

1. Motor room   3. Staircase   5. Lobby   7. Plant room
2. Bathroom   4. Office   6. Void

The internal staircase in the IT room, pictured right, is formed by poured concrete and underlit lozenge-shaped glass treads. The building is wired for the latest IT, and all systems feed into a central 'brain', a spectacular glass-walled room at the heart of the building.

Cross section

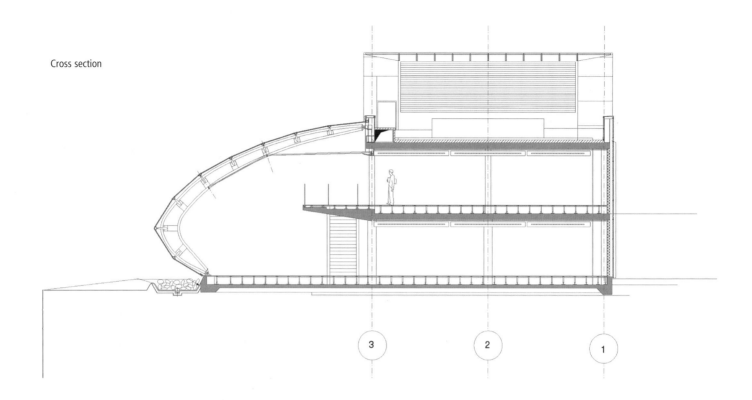

A curved coachbuilt riveted aluminum reception desk in the glazed area doubles as a juice and cappuccino bar, effectively mediating between public and private space. The company was keen to bring back a symbol of British '70's nostalgia: the uniformed tea lady with her trolley.

Dedicating particular attention to a traditionally neglected area of office design, the architect has designed mosaic-clad WCs that feature cast hand basins and electronic taps.

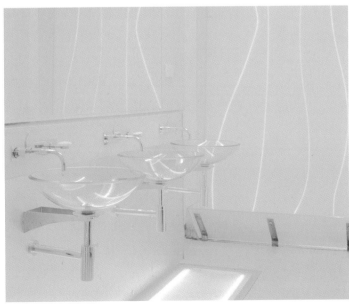

GC Osaka Building
Chuo, Osaka, Japan

The office building for GC, located in Osaka, is a fine example of wooden fire protection, adhering to functional requirements while maintaining a sense of aesthetic balance.

Following changes in the Japanese Building Standards Law, which regulates changes ranging from specification to performance standards, an attempt was made to ensure the required fire resistance by covering the steel structure with wood. A series of experiments led to the use of 25+25mm thick particle board, comprising a so-called 'flammable barrier' design. The wood used also acts as a finish, resulting in a reduction of costs and in the use of resources.

This six-floor building structure is made up of one-story-high Vierendeel trusses, each of which spans 22 m, on every other floor. Small rooms, such as the library/information corner and the training and dining rooms, are located on the floors with trusses, while large rooms, such as the showroom and a large, continuous office space, have been placed on the column-free floors.

The building has an elegant glass curtain wall, making the structural system completely visible even from the exterior and bringing the maximum amount of natural light into the work spaces.

Internal circulation routes are complemented by a long external metal staircase, which serves as a possible fire escape and which is connected to the upper floors on each landing by a sunny communal terrace.

Photographs: Hiroyuki Hirai

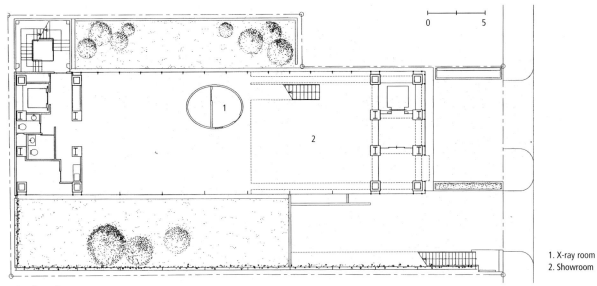

First floor plan

1. X-ray room
2. Showroom

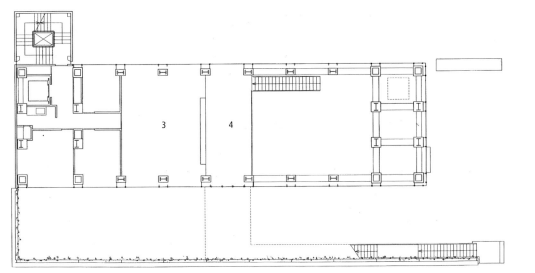

Second floor plan

3. Dining room
4. Library /
   Information corner

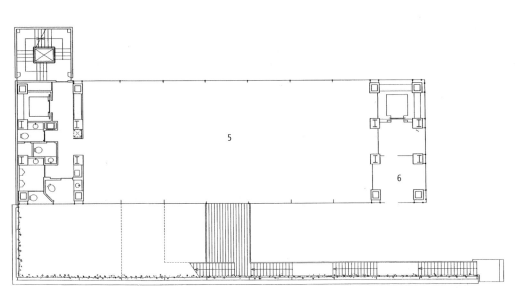

Third floor plan

5. Office
6. Reception room

With a steel structure wrapped in wood, this office building is a good example of newly developed wooden fire protection building methods. A series of preliminary experiments led to the use of 25+25mm thick particle board, comprising a so-called 'flammable barrier' design and simultaneously acting as a finish.

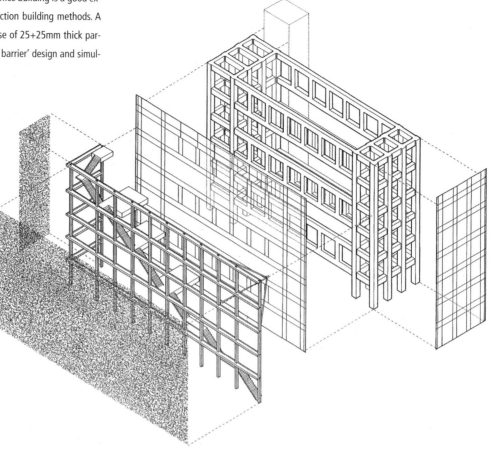

Cross section

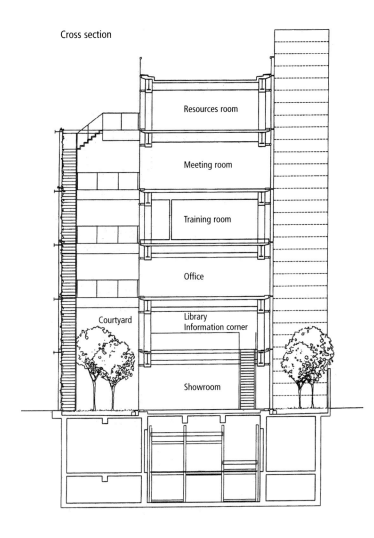

Resources room

Meeting room

Training room

Office

Library
Information corner

Courtyard

Showroom

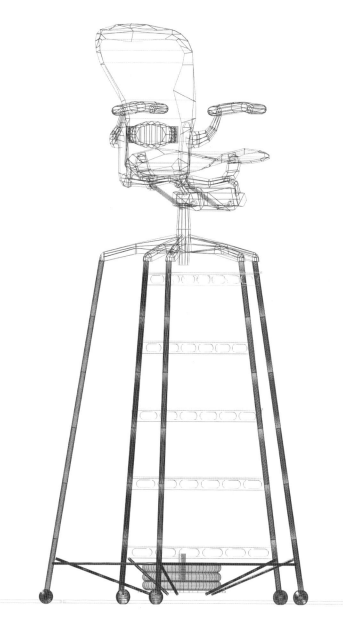

designblue
The Oxo Tower]
London, UK

The designblue studio is a somewhat unusual space and is the joint design work of Richard Palmer (RCA) and Dr. Phil Green. Together they form designblue, with a strong view on what a successful design should be; the studio is a personal statement to this effect.

The designblue studio is a relatively small space and measures just 6 x 4 m on the plan view, with a ceiling height at 3.2 m, a complete glass frontage and a floor to ceiling mirror on the rear wall. On a practical level, the design focuses on creating a vertical separation between private and shared space in such a small studio.

By placing the desk at a height of 2.1 m, and the chairs at 2 m to match, the design workstations are kept distinctively private, and this elevated position creates a feeling of controlled isolation. Any confidential information that is left on the desk is also kept out of view of onlookers that walk past the studio.

The shared space below is deliberately designed to create a feeling of openness that is enhanced by the clever use of the mirror in combination with the tubular structures placed in the corners. These provide much needed storage space, but visually emphasize the effect of the mirror; to invite you into the reflected space. A light wall under the wing-shaped desk illuminates the studio through the open frame structures of the pedestal chairs and is reflected on the underside of the wing-shaped desk, giving this substantial structure a less oppressive look.

Photographs: Ruth Julia Gough & Simon Jarret

The vertical separation of the two working areas provides a strong feeling of privacy, although the two areas are easily within audible distance.

By placing the desk at a height of 2.1 m, and the chairs at 2 meters to match, the design work stations are kept distinctively private, and this elevated position creates a feeling of controlled isolation.

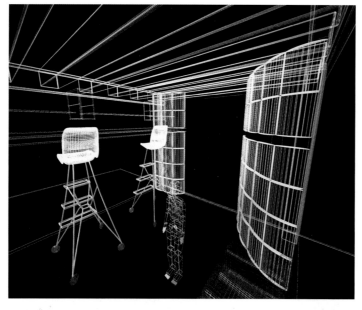
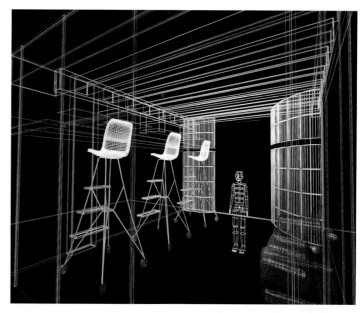

A light wall under the wing-shaped desk illuminates the studio through the open frame structures of the pedestal chairs and is reflected on the underside of the wing-shaped desk, giving this substantial structure a less oppressive appearance.

Nickl & Partner Architekten
Lindberghatelier
Munich, Germany

The objective of the program was to design a building whose structure and flexibility would reflect the needs and demands of the future tenants, whilst at the same time harmonizing outwardly with the as yet unfinished but essentially heterogeneous nature of the surrounding development.

The result is a simple cube. Anchored by its head –the entrance area– to the Lindberghstrasse in the south, the body of the building appears to almost float into the landscape. The rather raw industrial character of the outer skin has an optically defensive effect that belies the openness enjoyed by the occupants.

The clear geometry of the building is split into four distinct levels, the various elements being linked in their vertical axis by the closed stairwells. A car park devoid of external walls affords 18 spaces for cars and service vehicles as well as room for bicycles. The basement itself is composed of the archive and adjoining rooms, reached by way of the staff entrance.

The entrance area contains communal facilities such as kitchen, staff room and foyer. The office and workshop area is openly planned to allow future tenants maximum flexibility to create their own working space.

The first floor in its entirety is home to the architectural offices of Nickl + Partner Architekten GmbH, these being composed of the architectural workshop with two special use areas, and a central area containing service and information facilities.

The two head ends of the floor are occupied respectively by the management offices and competition department to the north, and reception and conference facilities to the south, the functional division of the offices being defined by moveable partitions and the illuminated boxes of the central area.

The roof area supports sufficient vegetation to create the desired 'green thumb' effect of the development plan. A partly covered roof terrace forms the topmost part of the building and offers additional recreational facilities for the staff.

The future addition of an extra story to the building is also an option. The whole shell of the building was planned in pre-cast elements, allowing a reduction of the total construction time to 10 months.

Photographs: Stefan Müller-Naumann

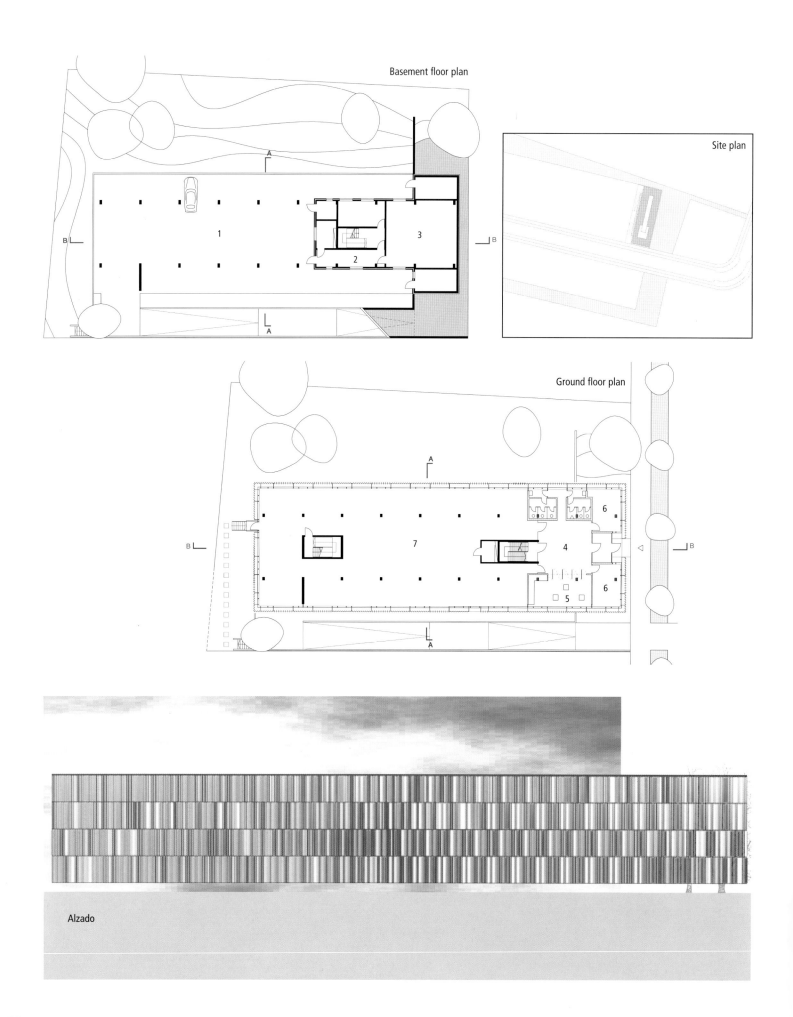

Basement floor plan

Site plan

Ground floor plan

Alzado

First floor plan

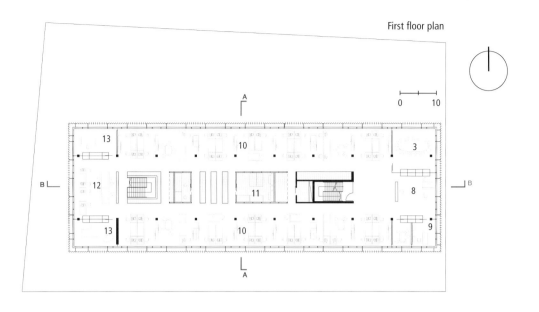

0   10

1. Open parking area
2. Internal entrance
3. Storeroom
4. Hall
5. Canteen
6. Meeting room
7. Office and workshop area
8. Reception
9. Secretaries' office
10. Architecture workshop
11. Service area, kitchen, model building, library,
    IT product info
12. Competition department
13. Management

Roof floor plan

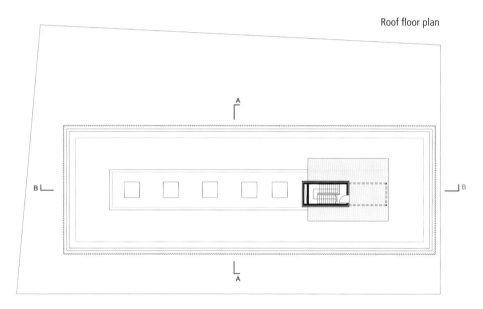

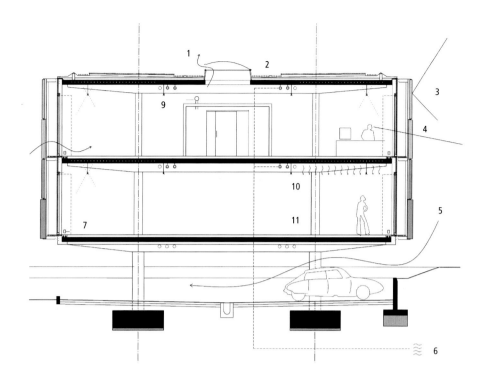

Section AA
Thermal conditioning diagram

1. Used air
2. Extensive vegetation
3. Individual shade
4. View
5. Naturally ventilated parking area
6. Cooling with ground water
7. Connector heating
8. Ventilation
9. Mechanically ventilated service area
10. Concrete core heating regulation
11. Summer cooling, winter heating

Section BB

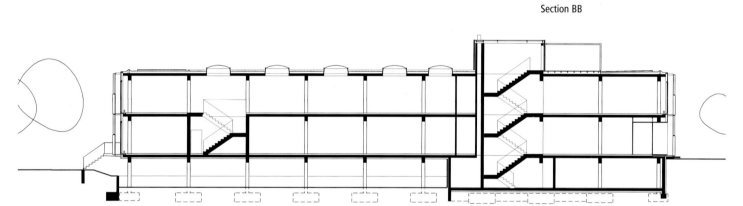

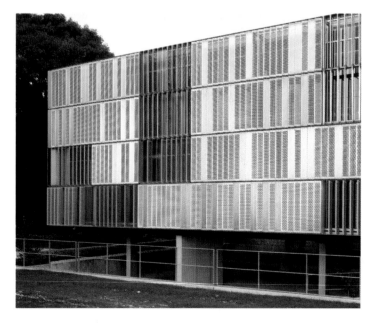

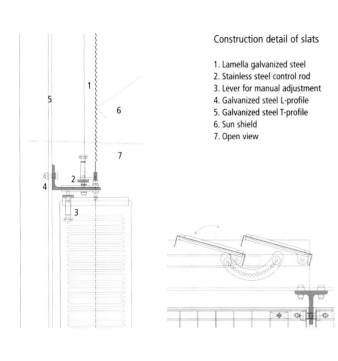

Construction detail of slats

1. Lamella galvanized steel
2. Stainless steel control rod
3. Lever for manual adjustment
4. Galvanized steel L-profile
5. Galvanized steel T-profile
6. Sun shield
7. Open view

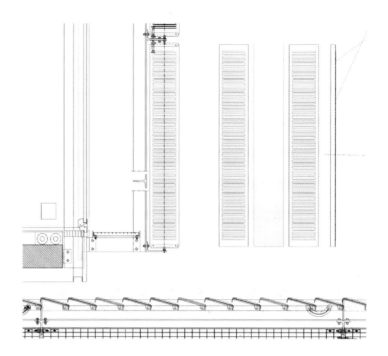

The alternating pattern of industrial glass and rough steel lamella defines the look of the building – a unique and, with varying light conditions, constantly changing skin. Each block of lamella is unique in its pattern of glass and steel elements, reflecting the individuality of the work spaces hidden within. Each lamella field can be adjusted manually by means of a rod rather like a french window shutter. Horizontal order combined with vertical rotation make the shimmering skin of the building appear both open and closed at the same time.

Nykredit Headquarters
Copenhagen, Denmark

Danish practice Schmidt Hammer & Lassen's headquarters for Nykredit is by far the finest new building on Copenhagen's waterfront. Seen from the outside, the building is an enormous cube facing the water. Each side is slightly different. One enters from the elevation parallel to the water. The low-ceilinged foyer has an aura of 1960's glamour and spectacular pieces by artists Per Kierkeby and Anita Jørgensen line the reception area.

Stairs lead up to the first floor to enter the principal atrium. The company's 300-seat cafeteria is located on this floor. Suspended in the air above are walkways linking the upper floors and wenge-clad meeting 'boxes' that project out into the atrium void. From here, the two blocks of office accommodation are clearly visible. These are all laid out according to a 'new way of working' philosophy, with open plans, glass boxes for quiet work and flexible wiring. Management suites and the accounts department are separately located on the two platforms spanning the atrium at a high level.

By raising the main atrium space one floor above street level, using the low reception as a buffer zone, the architect has overcome the problematic presence of the main road outside.

Photographs: Jørgen True and Søren Kuhn

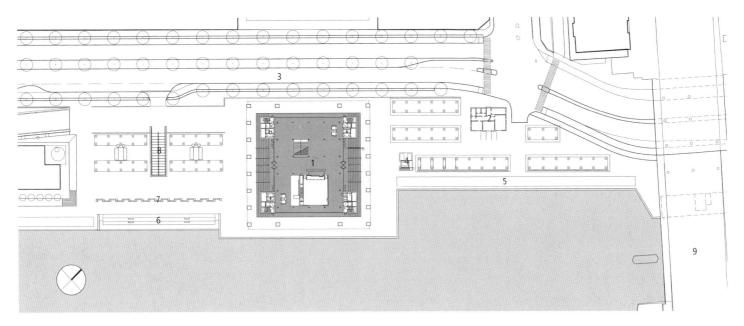

Site plan

1. Nykredit - New Headquarters
2. Toldbygningen (former Customs House)
3. Kalvedbod Brygge
4. Service building
5. Promenade
6. Water stairs
7. Stone ornament by Per Kierkeby
8. Ramp to parking area
9. Langebro

In interplay with aviaries and the sound of water from the water sculpture by the auditorium, vegetation constitutes an additional 'organic' dimension in the straight lines of architecture.

Under the large round skylights, the atrium connects the open and flexible eight-story administration areas of the two flanking office sections. Suspended 'meeting boxes' sided with dark wenge wood create a dynamic effect in the bright atrium, accentuating the meeting room as an important common function.

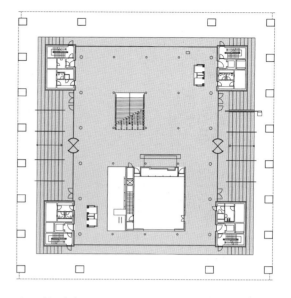

Ground level plan

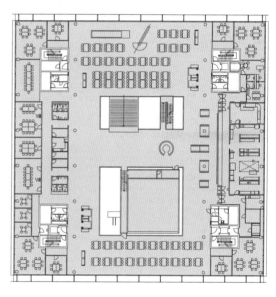

First floor plan

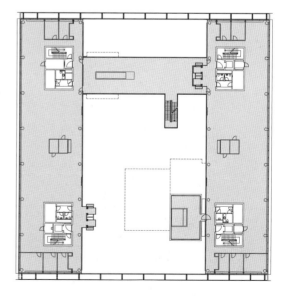

Seventh floor plan

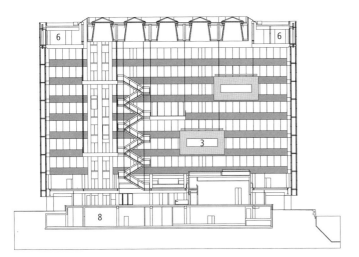

Section AA

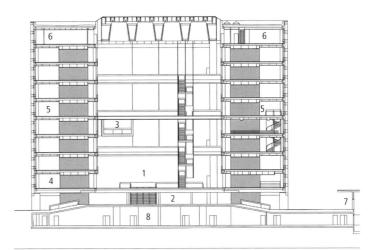

Section BB

1. Atrium, canteen
2. Lobby, entrance
3. Meeting box
4. Meeting section
5. Open office space
6. Management floor
7. Service building
8. Basement

The meeting rooms, which have been designed as boxes, are fastened to the rows of columns, and –with built-in vibration absorbers– suspended from the roof or footbridges. A wide stairway rises in a combination of lightweight and transparency as well as monumentality from the entrance floor towards the light and drama of the atrium.

de architectengroep
(design: Bjarne Mastenbroek / Miguel Loos)]

de architectengroep Office Building
Amsterdam, The Netherlands

The conversion of an old factory in Amsterdam provided this office building for de Architectengroep. The original building was built at the beginning of the 20th century and served as a flour mill that supplied the Amsterdam bakeries. The mills moved out of the city center in the 1950's and the building was converted into office space.

In 1996, de Architectengroep moved in and the whole building was stripped on the inside, laying bare the old concrete structure and the original massive wooden floors.

The new interiors were designed to make minimal additions to the old structure. On the north side the building originally had no floors, but contained vertical storage silos. In this part of the building new vertical voids were created, both to serve as a visual connection between floors, and as a reminiscence of the old silos.

During the later renovation of the ground floor in 2000, the need for more space became urgent and so the demolition of a low-quality 1970's extension was halted.

The steel beams were kept and a wooden frame with skylights was put on top. All the 'freedom' these elements have was exploited, i.e. different standard sizes and colors. The terrace and garden was designed in collaboration with Annemiek Diekman, a Dutch landscape architect.

Photographs: Christian Richters

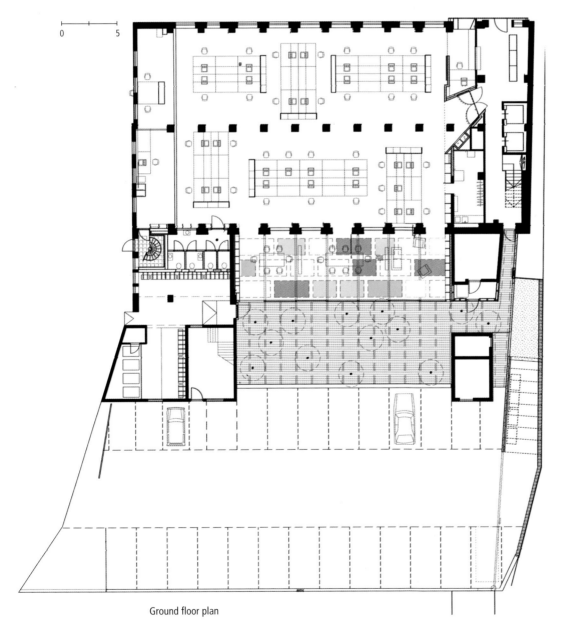

Ground floor plan

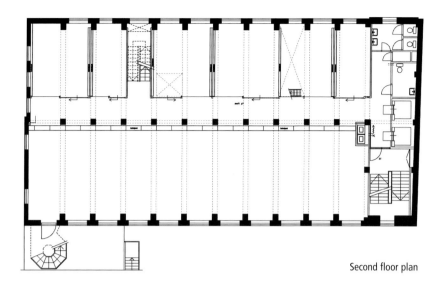

Second floor plan

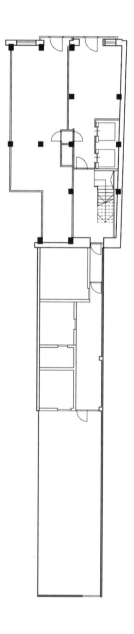

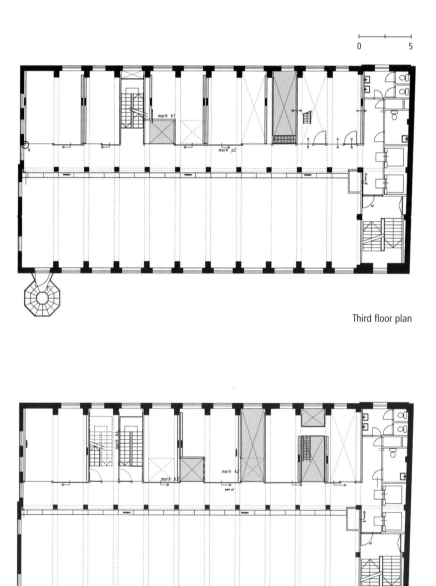

Third floor plan

Fourth floor plan

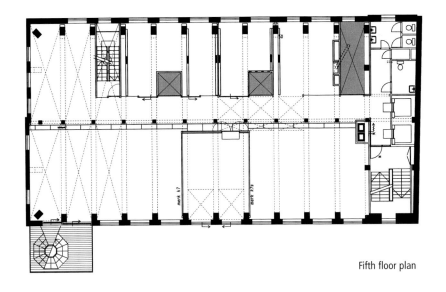

Fifth floor plan

0   5

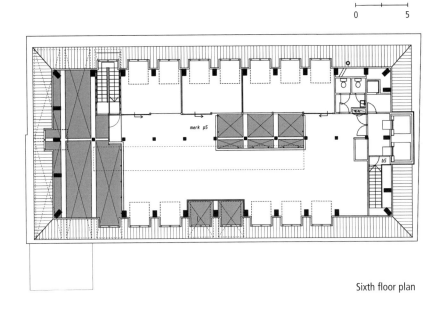

Sixth floor plan

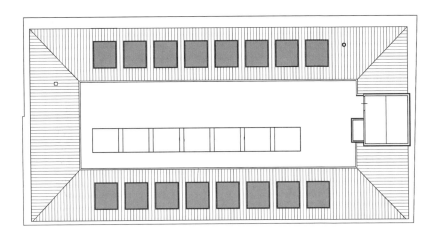

Roof floor plan

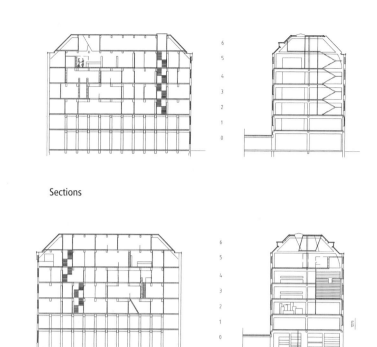

Sections

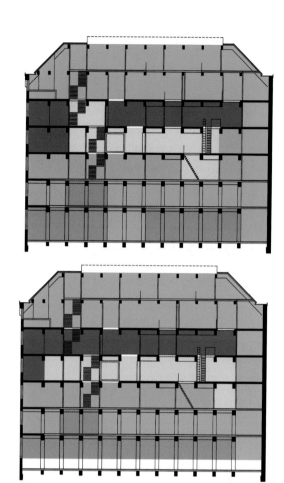

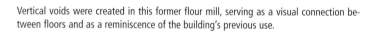

Vertical voids were created in this former flour mill, serving as a visual connection be-tween floors and as a reminiscence of the building's previous use.

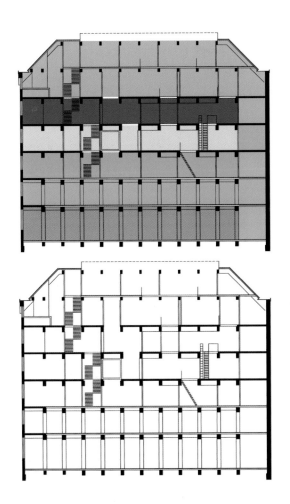
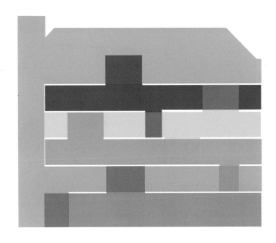
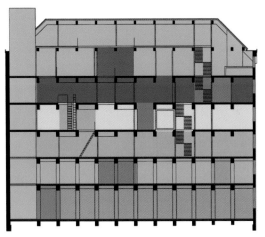

Priestman Architects
Ted Baker Headquarters
London, UK

Witty and inventive, these London head offices for the fashion design company, Ted Baker plc, creatively recolonize a former post office building. Matthew Preistman Architects were commissioned to remodel the 40,000 ft² premises. A conventional mixture of offices, meeting rooms, showrooms and a staff canteen was required, but these also had to reflect the underlying informal philosophy of the company.

The entry is signposted by a huge lobster billboard, an instant graphic landmark. The route to the upper levels is animated by a linear history of Ted Baker displays. Existing lift cages go up to the third-floor reception area, revealing the spectacular interiors.

The central, triangular courtyard has been covered with a glazed roof to add space and light. Configured around the courtyard, the second and third floors are large open-plan areas for showrooms, workstations and meeting rooms. Stairs lead down from the office level to the lower floor. The staff canteen occupies the center of the courtyard, surrounded by bands of showrooms enclosed by sliding canvas and stainless-steel screens. The original canal-side cladding has been replaced with glazed sliding doors that lead on to cedar-clad balconies.

The building has been stripped back to its bare shell, with exposed sandblasted structures. The existing concrete floor screed has been sealed, with traces of the original floor surfaces and partitions still faintly visible. All building services are routed from the ceiling or perimeter walls, so that workspaces can be adapted to individual needs.

Photographs: David Glandorge

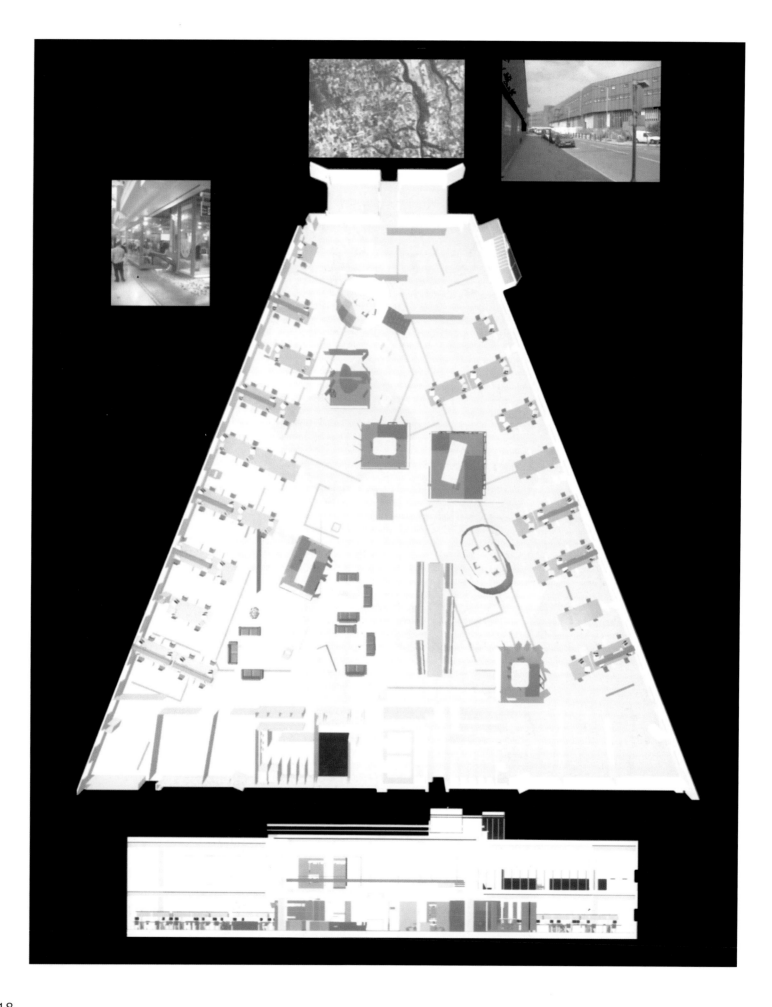

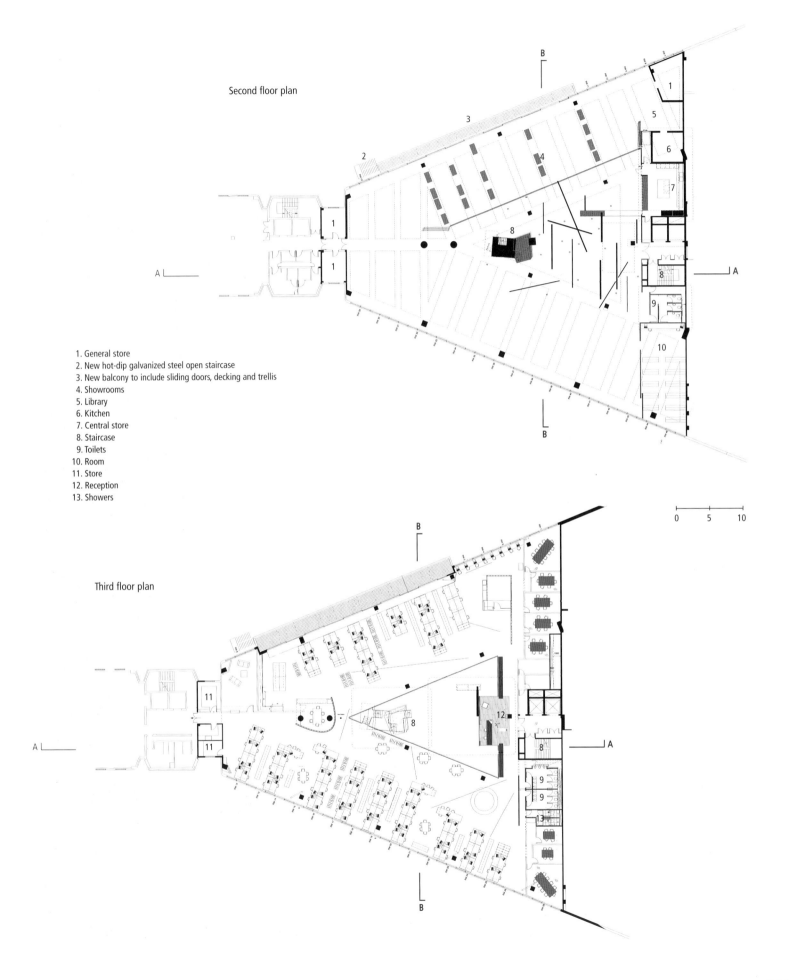

Second floor plan

1. General store
2. New hot-dip galvanized steel open staircase
3. New balcony to include sliding doors, decking and trellis
4. Showrooms
5. Library
6. Kitchen
7. Central store
8. Staircase
9. Toilets
10. Room
11. Store
12. Reception
13. Showers

Third floor plan

0   5   10

Section BB

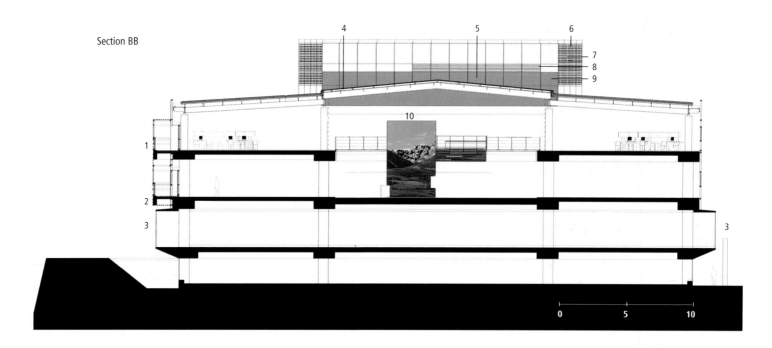

Section AA

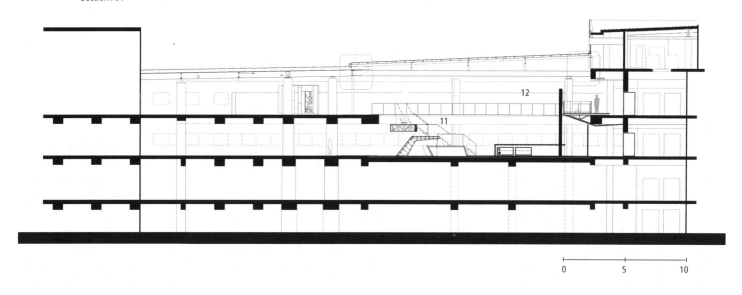

1. Cedar slatting rails, trellis and shading to existing
   and proposed balcony
2. New balcony
3. New glazing by freeholder
4. New glazed roof to courtyard
5. New replacement cladding to front
6. Approximately 12 m² of aluminum louvers to M&E
   specification; design and quantity to M&E specification.
7. New grills
8. Existing grills
9. Shaded section
10. Double height wall
11. Staircase
12. Reception

40,000 ft² head offices for retailer Ted Baker plc, with reception areas, showrooms, meeting rooms, a staff canteen and extensive alterations to the external fabric, including atrium glazing, of the former postal sorting office. The outside of the building facing the street is unaltered, whilst the interiors are open, creative and forward-thinking. Quirky, yet with an inventive approach to materials and space handling, this makeover seeks to crystallize the company philosophy.

Carlos Manzano y Asociados
Jazztel Lisboa
Lisboa, Portugal

When the architects remodeled this 7,000 m former grain store, the project established the hierarchical structure of a city, with two districts –the urban extension and the garden city–, an avenue, a square and a port. The structure of two inclined volumes forms the entrance to the city. The widest part of the office represents the urban extension. A perpendicular arrangement of work positions makes up the blocks of houses, only interrupted by the avenue.

At the end of this route is the square, a place for reunions and rest from the office. The garden city is the management area. White volumes with marked edges stand out against the slate floor and organize the space by creating different work areas.

Once the space on the ground plan was structured, the subject of height was considered. Here micro architecture has been the answer: small sections that interrupt the view and mark out the workspaces. On the ground floor, solid bodies hold the offices and on the upper floor they hold the meeting rooms: elevated and open micro squares over the city. The south end of the building comprises the reunion and rest areas; this is the city port. Its polished concrete floor marks the limit with the workspaces. With regard to the original store framework, the façade has been moved like a more permeable double inner skin, overlooking the Tajo river.

Photographs: Sergio Mah

127

The building is a large container in which the 130 x 26 m structure is the great protagonist. With a marked industrial feel, the 26 m reinforced concrete roof trusses cover the space that is supported by large pillars along the north and south façades, creating a strong rhythm.

The work positions are placed in a perpendicular arrangement on the upper floor, thus forming city blocks.

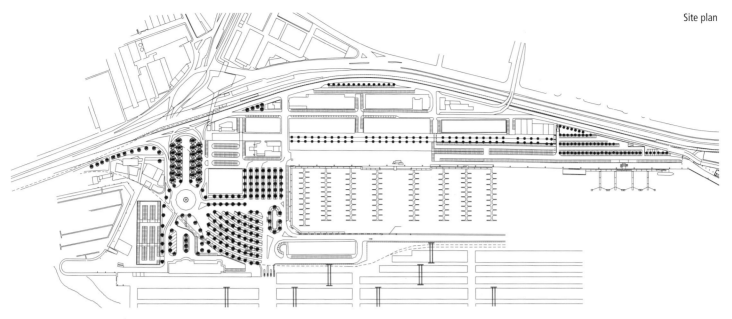

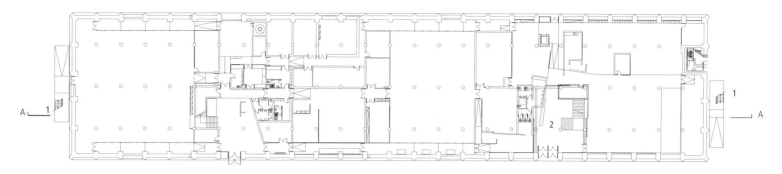

Ground floor plan

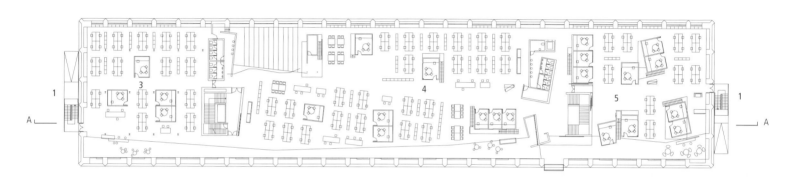

Upper floor plan

1. Emergency stairs
2. Reception
3. Technical area
4. Marketing and sales
5. Corporate area

The architect has confronted and organized the space as though it were a large metropolis: building avenues, arranging the traffic, siting emblematic buildings, etc. He has focussed the work from a bird's-eye view. Thus, Manzano's project presents an imaginative and orderly city that not only breaks down the strong pre-existing geometric imposition of the building, but also acquires its own autonomy.

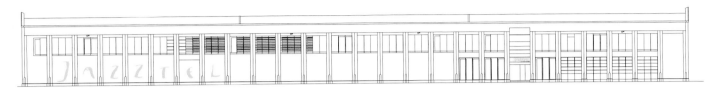

South elevation

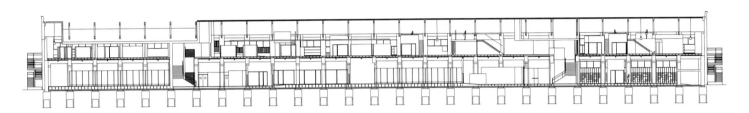

Section AA

A new height has been created on the upper floor containing other workspaces, like islands. This height commands a view over the outskirts.

The areas reserved for large numbers, such as the auditorium and the meeting room, retain the transparency and austerity of the building. This reaffirms the idea of open and linked spaces.

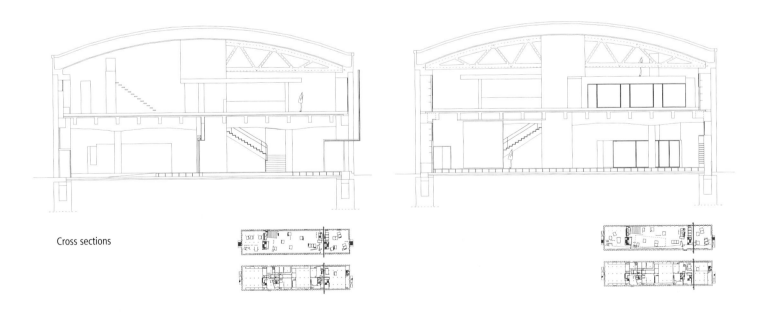

Cross sections

White Design
VELUX Sales Office & Training Centre
Kettering, UK

White Design Architects were commissioned to design the new regional sales office and training facility in Kettering, UK for window manufacturer Velux. The client's brief specified that the building was to act as a showcase for Velux products and demonstrate good environmental practice on a commercial basis. This inventive, three-story landmark building with sloping façades, functions both as an operational office and as a visitor's center for the public and construction professionals.

The innovative design combines high quality design with leading edge technology to minimize energy consumption. Natural cross ventilation and maximum use of daylight ensure increased user comfort and productivity, and reduced energy requirement.

The structure is a timber glue-laminated frame supported by a concrete base at ground and first floor. The roof folds around the main structure, almost touching the ground (slate on one side and cedar shingles on the other). The Velux windows on the upper levels are installed with rain and solar sensors that open and close windows and blinds.

Inside, White Design has taken its inspiration from the household attic – white walls, sloping roof, warm timber and spiral staircase. At the entrance, an elliptical rotunda acts as an organizing device with stairs wrapped around it and the bridge to the double-height boardroom protruding from it. At the base of the rotunda is a reception that commands the entrance hall.

Photographs: David Cross and Willmont Dixon & Waterhouse Design

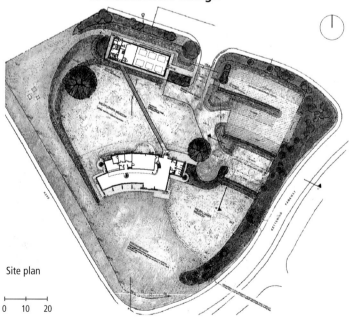

Site plan

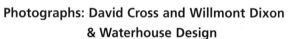

0   10   20

Site plan

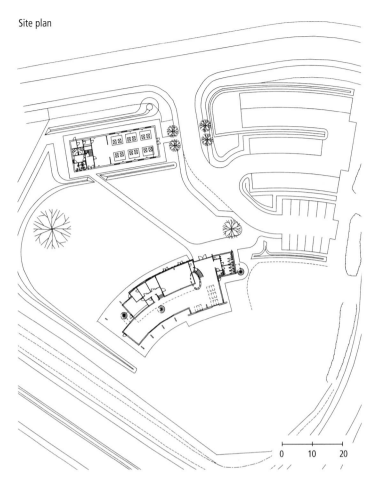

Window maker Velux required the building to have plenty of roof surface to act as a showcase for its products. For its Kettering office, White Design gave the company a roof that almost touches the ground. Seen from the main road, the 'roof' building is a good advertisement for Velux – using 95 of its windows.

1. Entrance
2. Reception
3 .Display / exhibition
4. Kitchen / staff room
5. Plant room
6. Electrical plant / services
7. Store
8. Lobby
9. Meeting room
10. Bathroom
11. Void
12. Open plan office
13. Office
14. Cloaks / store
15. Bridge
16. Boardroom
17. Services

Ground floor plan

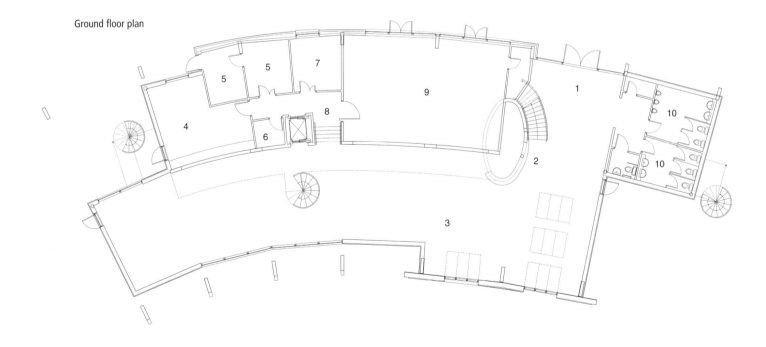

First floor plan

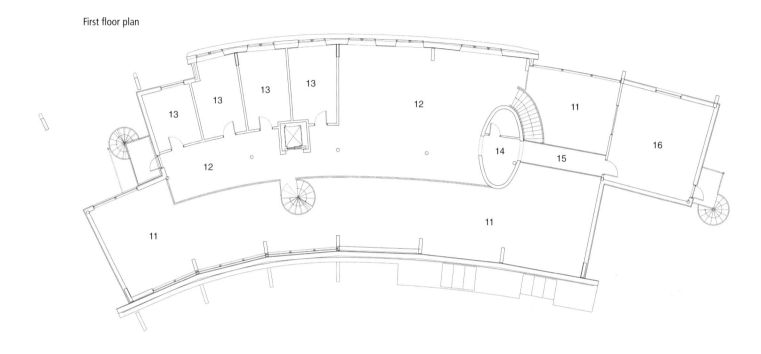

Second floor plan

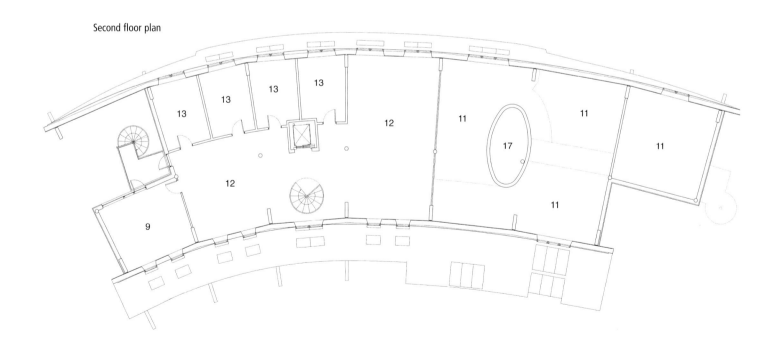

Section AA

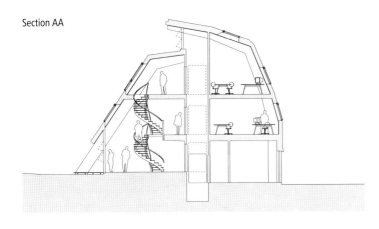

Section BB

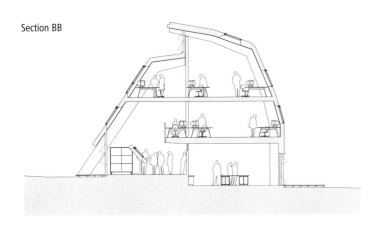

Section CC

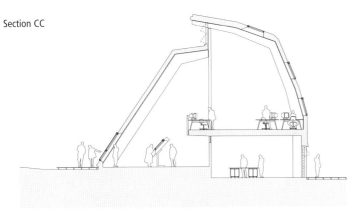

Section DD

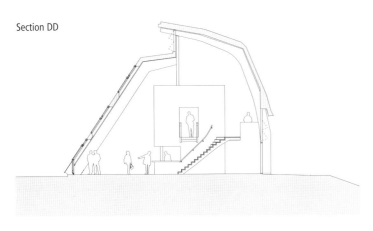

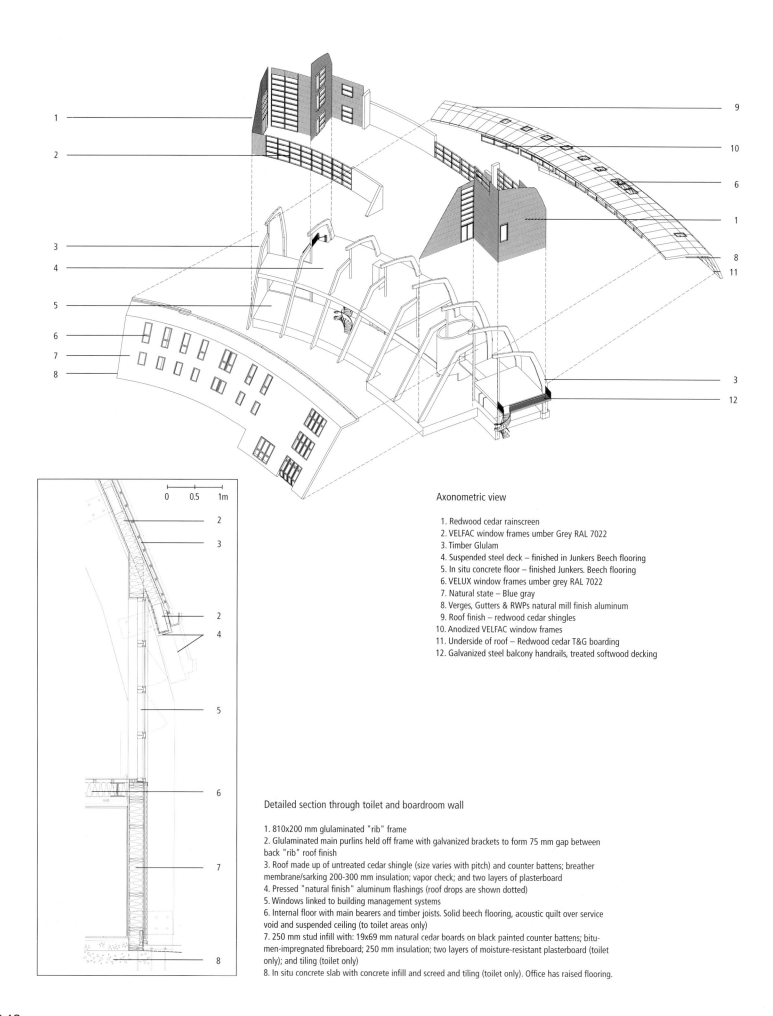

Axonometric view

1. Redwood cedar rainscreen
2. VELFAC window frames umber Grey RAL 7022
3. Timber Glulam
4. Suspended steel deck – finished in Junkers Beech flooring
5. In situ concrete floor – finished Junkers. Beech flooring
6. VELUX window frames umber grey RAL 7022
7. Natural state – Blue gray
8. Verges, Gutters & RWPs natural mill finish aluminum
9. Roof finish – redwood cedar shingles
10. Anodized VELFAC window frames
11. Underside of roof – Redwood cedar T&G boarding
12. Galvanized steel balcony handrails, treated softwood decking

0   0.5   1m

Detailed section through toilet and boardroom wall

1. 810x200 mm glulaminated "rib" frame
2. Glulaminated main purlins held off frame with galvanized brackets to form 75 mm gap between back "rib" roof finish
3. Roof made up of untreated cedar shingle (size varies with pitch) and counter battens; breather membrane/sarking 200-300 mm insulation; vapor check; and two layers of plasterboard
4. Pressed "natural finish" aluminum flashings (roof drops are shown dotted)
5. Windows linked to building management systems
6. Internal floor with main bearers and timber joists. Solid beech flooring, acoustic quilt over service void and suspended ceiling (to toilet areas only)
7. 250 mm stud infill with: 19x69 mm natural cedar boards on black painted counter battens; bitumen-impregnated fibreboard; 250 mm insulation; two layers of moisture-resistant plasterboard (toilet only); and tiling (toilet only)
8. In situ concrete slab with concrete infill and screed and tiling (toilet only). Office has raised flooring.

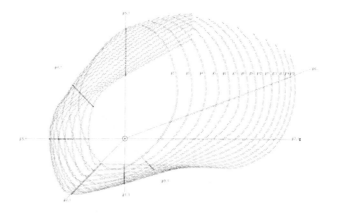

Lorcan O'Herlihy Architects & Pugh + Scarpa Architects]
YouBet.com Headquarters
San Fernando Valley, USA

Two California practices, Lorcan O'Herlihy Architects and Pugh+Scarpa Architects, were commissioned to remodel an existing 35,000 ft² building located in a San Fernando Valley office park into the corporate headquarters of YouBet.com, an online wagering company.

The design includes a Data Center, the rectilinear core of the project, surrounded by an open plan of workstations, conference rooms, and offices. The client had a specific request for security, which created the need for a lounge area at the reception desk, which could be isolated from the rest of the offices. The Data Center is clad in curved acrylic panels which are illuminated from behind expressing the mainframe computers and network systems contained within.

The workstations are nontraditional in appearance with translucent panels that further accentuate the open environment of the offices. Conference rooms float between the workstations as highly visible sculptural pieces. The main conference room, adjacent to the cafeteria, is a translucent box of reglit glass with large translucent glazed sliding doors. This room can be opened completely to the cafeteria, or closed for the most important meetings of the company. The perimeter of the plan is lined with private offices with exterior views, reserved for the upper management of the company.

Architecturally, the space helps to define the fast paced, high-risk, and progressive attitudes of the company, its staff, and the services that they provide.

Photographs: Marvin Rand

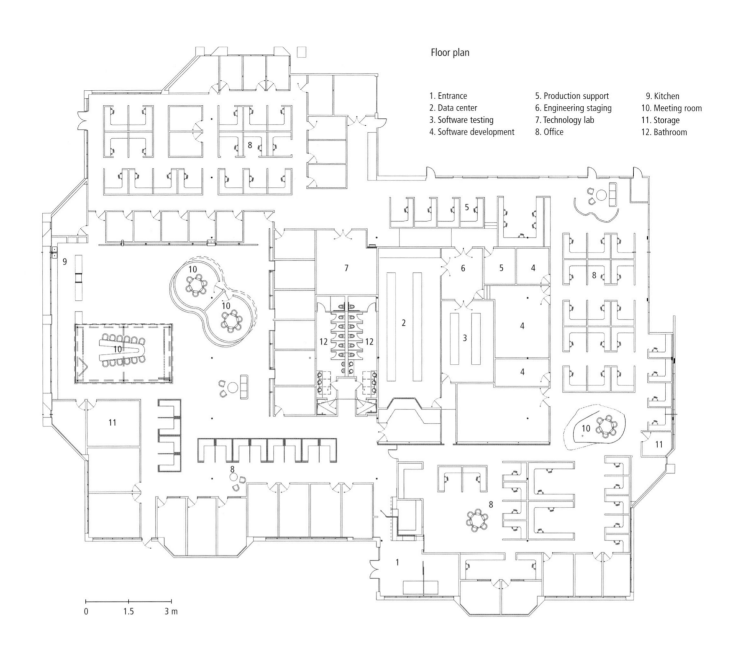

Floor plan

1. Entrance
2. Data center
3. Software testing
4. Software development
5. Production support
6. Engineering staging
7. Technology lab
8. Office
9. Kitchen
10. Meeting room
11. Storage
12. Bathroom

0   1.5   3 m

The building was stripped back to the essential shell, revealing a wooden ceiling of joists and laminated boarding, thin columns and a bare concrete floor which, with all its defects, was simply sealed and polished. Translucent panels contain open workstations, and long acrylic panels, curved in cross-section and set horizontally, enclose the data center. Illuminated from behind, these panels form glowing corrugated walls. Ultimately this scheme has to do with the architects' pleasure in materials and light, and in juxtaposition of the rough and refined.

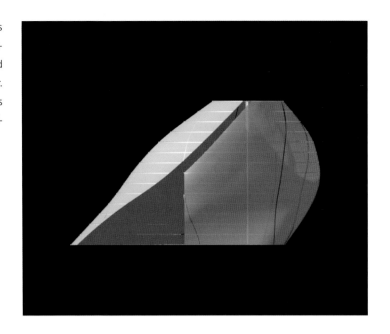

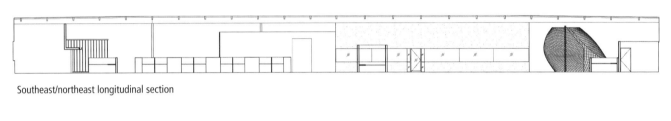

Southeast/northeast longitudinal section

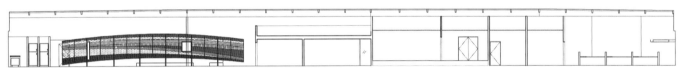

Southwest/northwest longitudinal section

Ramón Llopart Ricart
Radio Barcelona
Barcelona, Spain

In architectural terms, the rehabilitation of Radio Barcelona goes beyond the building's physical alterations to become a prototype of regeneration in its field. This is demonstrated by the versatility of the different environments, multi-functionality of space, volumetric spaciousness that avoids closed compartments, the democratic and homogenized treatment of finishings, etc. This new concept consists of projecting a control center surrounded by the main studios. An idea of space hitherto unknown in the world of radio. So, by means of a closed-circuit television, there is communication with the other studios in the radio station. These are:

- Toresky Studio: a multi-functional studio for radio and television with all the possibilities of a great container for events, recording and audience.

- Caspe Studio: a studio that is visible from the street and is conceived as a multi-purpose studio -a 'radio boutique'- capable of broadcasting any of the programs or producing particular promotions. It is Radio Barcelona's showcase.

- News Studio: located on the first floor, with a direct view from the news section and connected by closed-circuit television to the control center, so that news may be broadcasted without the need to go down to the studio area.

Finally, and taking the ground floor at street level as a reference, this historic and emblematic point of union with the city opens some areas to the public, such as the vestibule, the Toresky Studio and the Caspe Studio.

The greatest techological potential, both in building technique and multimedia installations, is concentrated on the roof and in the basement. In the intermediate areas, above the offices and below the ground floor studios, we find workspaces where everything has been thought of to offer maximum comfort in a working environment.

Design team: M. Vila, C. Fernández, X. Amat, B. Bertrán, C. Guri, C. Casajuana, M. Ruiz & M. Panero

Photographs: Joan Mundó

Main facade

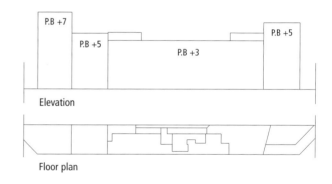

Elevation

Floor plan

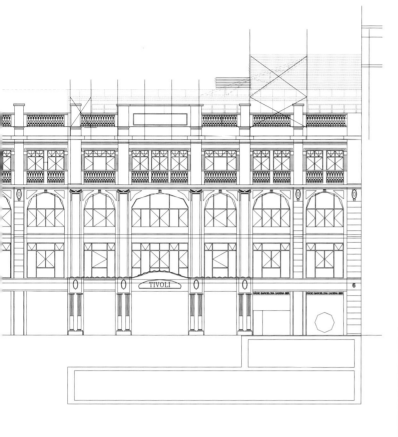

Main facade. Roof

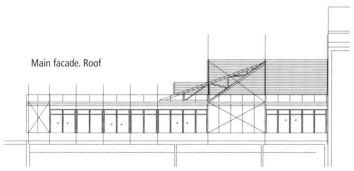

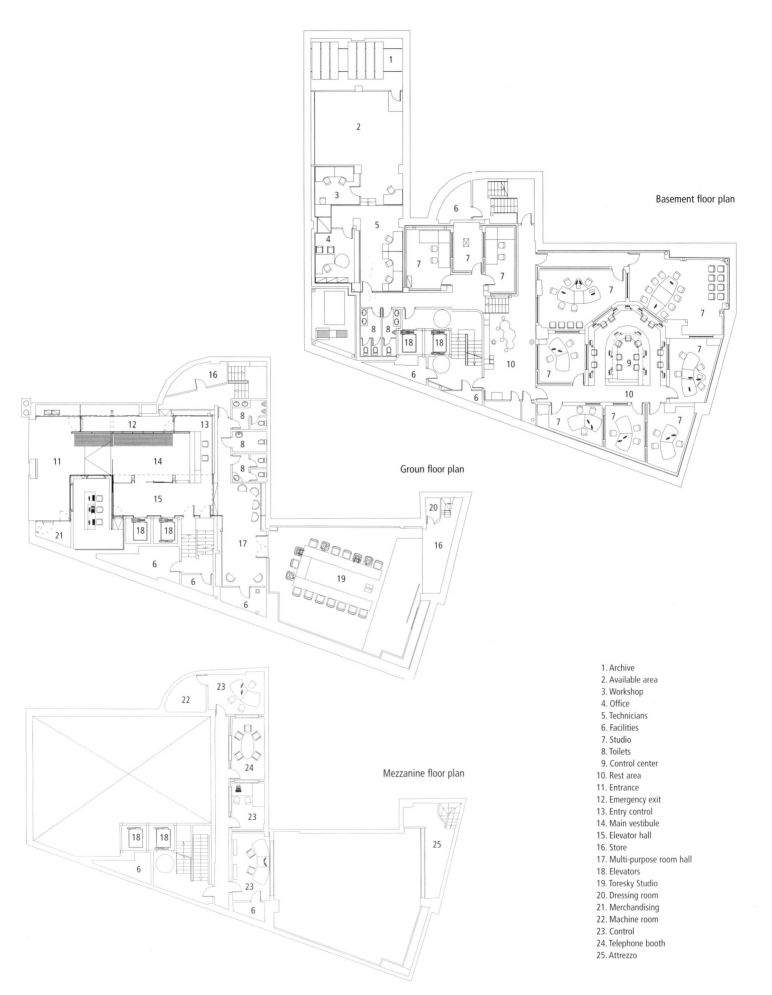

Basement floor plan

Groun floor plan

Mezzanine floor plan

1. Archive
2. Available area
3. Workshop
4. Office
5. Technicians
6. Facilities
7. Studio
8. Toilets
9. Control center
10. Rest area
11. Entrance
12. Emergency exit
13. Entry control
14. Main vestibule
15. Elevator hall
16. Store
17. Multi-purpose room hall
18. Elevators
19. Toresky Studio
20. Dressing room
21. Merchandising
22. Machine room
23. Control
24. Telephone booth
25. Attrezzo

First floor plan

Second floor plan

6. Facilities
8. Toilets
12. Emergency exit
18. Elevators
26. Office
27. Program management
28. Program area
29. Training classrooms
30. Meeting room
31. Creative area
32. Booth
33. News Studio
34. Radio formulas
35. Marketing
36. Reception
37. News management

38. Contents management
39. News area
40. Advanced areas
41. Terrace
42. Marketing management
43. Commercial area
44. Administration and sales
45. Sales area
46. Administration
47. General management
48. Boardroom
49. Meeting room
50. Cadena Ser management
51. General management secretary
52. Radio Barcelona management

In the intermediate areas of the building, we find workspaces where everything has been thought of to offer maximum comfort in a working environment. This is demonstrated by the space segmentation with a view of other areas; also in the areas set side for relaxation, such as the terraces.

The architect has projected a great control center surrounded by the main studios that broadcast in AM, FM and up to four specialist and independent musical frequencies. The layout permits triangulation between the studios and control center, so that from any studio one can see the two adjacent ones and, opposite, the control center, obtaining an idea of space, hitherto unknown in the world of radio.

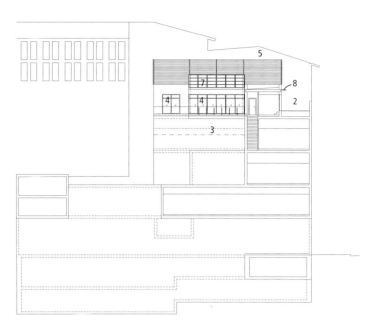

1. Haircol 59 de chapa colaborante roof forging and double layer finish de rasilla
2. Accessible terrace roof with IPE wood paving on supports
3. Rough-cast and painted finish
4. Black Technal aluminum carpentry
5. Acoustic facing of 20 cm granulated Oxirón grey lacquered strips
6. Glazed inclined roof
7. Acierod sandwich panel facing
8. Tubular and sheet metal eaves

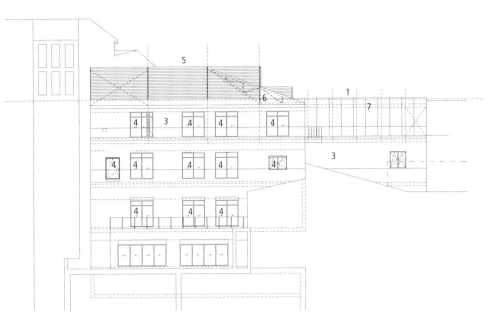

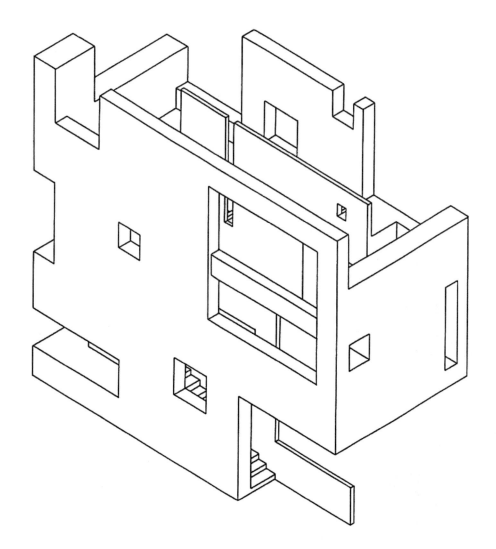

Claesson Koivisto Rune
Sony Music Headquarters
Stockholm, Sweden

Sony Music is one of the world's leading record companies and Sony Music Sweden is the largest in Sweden. Moving from a suburb to a central location in Stockholm, Sony Music holds an entire old building, previously used as a church. Six floors altogether, of which three constituted the church room with full ceiling height. The key to the interior architecture lies in an articulated staircase in this space.

Music, music at high volume and one stereo per employee. No wonder a traditional record company is all closed offices and corridors. But the modern organization called for more direct internal communication. The solution was a hybrid between an open and closed plan (and headphones). The project has combined a number of closed conference-, meeting- and listening-rooms and open space for workstations. Semi walls, freestanding wall units or cabinets divide the open workspaces into different departments (marketing, finances, etc.).

The big, open space with its two mezzanines created the necessary conditions to build an intricate spatial composition working both horizontally and vertically. Two longitudinal staircases connect the floors. Most of office storage was placed against the stair walls. When moving around the floors or up and down the stairs the space is constantly changing. Lines of vision open and close again.

The original architecture is generally left untouched. Old walls are gray while new are white. The architectural composition is complex but the detailing is very simple. Simple materials, no linings, skirtings or visible glass fixations, in order to create a contrast to the inevitable chaos around workstations.

Photographs: Åke E: Son Lindman

Three of the six floors of this former church constituted the church room, with full ceiling height. The key to the interior architecture of this project lies in an articulated staircase in this space.

The big, open space with its two mezzanines created the necessary conditions to build an intricate spatial composition working both horizontally and vertically. Two longitudinal staircases connect the floors. When moving around the floors or up and down the stairs the space is constantly changing, with lines of vision opening and closing again.

Elevation

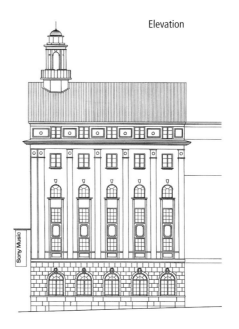

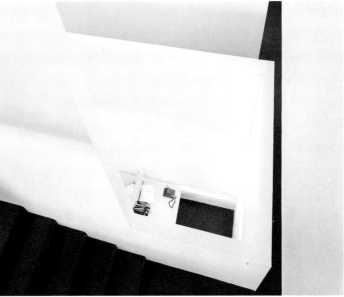

159

Second floor plan

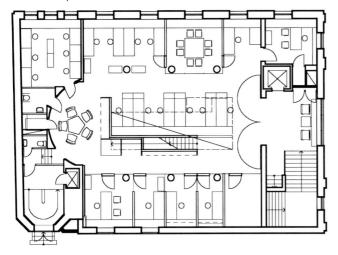

Lower ground floor plan

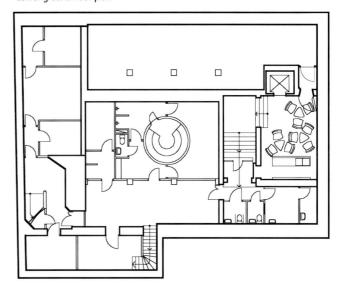

Third floor plan

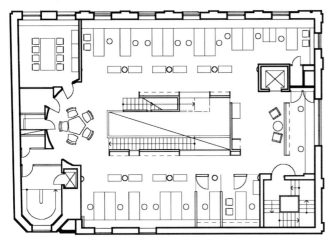

Ground floor plan

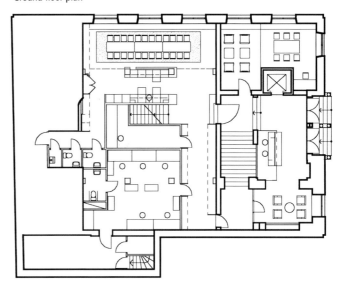

Fourth floor plan

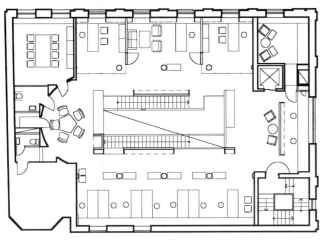

First floor plan

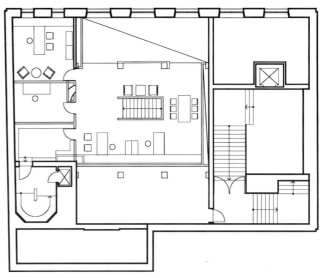

I.Net Headquarters
Milano, Italy

These Milan headquarters for the Internet services supplier, I.Net Group, were deliberately designed to avoid any physical representation of company functioning and performance. The architects, Cibic & Partners, developed various workspace and divider layouts, using degrees of transparency and colored opacity. The starting point in establishing the unique character of the office space was achieved also through use of special floors and ceilings to contain systems.

The 21,000 m² industrial building has six floors and each one is a sequence of fluid, dynamic, multicolored environments, small autonomous 'places' in their own right, intended to elicit emotional engagement by using unexpected situations to stimulate the senses and the imagination. The entry court is austerely sculpted and the reception area has a huge glass sheet as its back wall, while the relaxation room with its custom-made seats, table and chairs is an appropriately playful experience, and the cool minimalism of the stainless steel and white glass bar area is almost glacial.

The entrance can be considered the heart of the internal space of the ground floor. Two interconnected wings expand around the two central areas, which cover the six floors and where services and the elevator landing are located. The so-called 'technological' room is also on the ground floor, housing the central and electrical systems. The Web Farm consists of laboratories situated on the four central levels of the building. This space was created through use of foldable partitions in double-paned shatterproof glass.

Photographs: Santi Caleca

Second floor plan

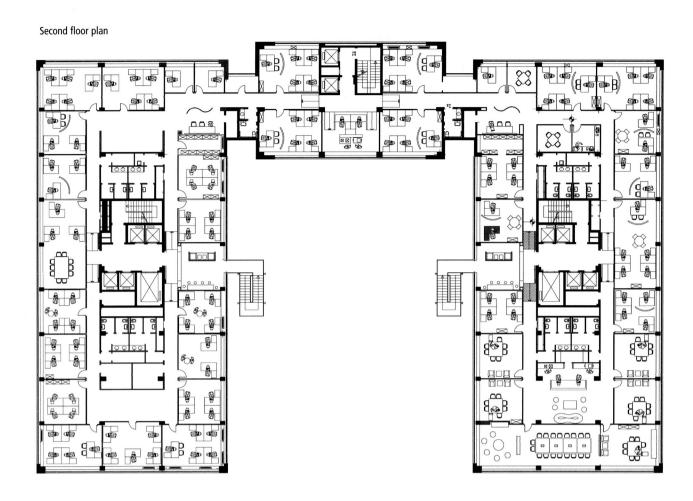

Ground floor plan

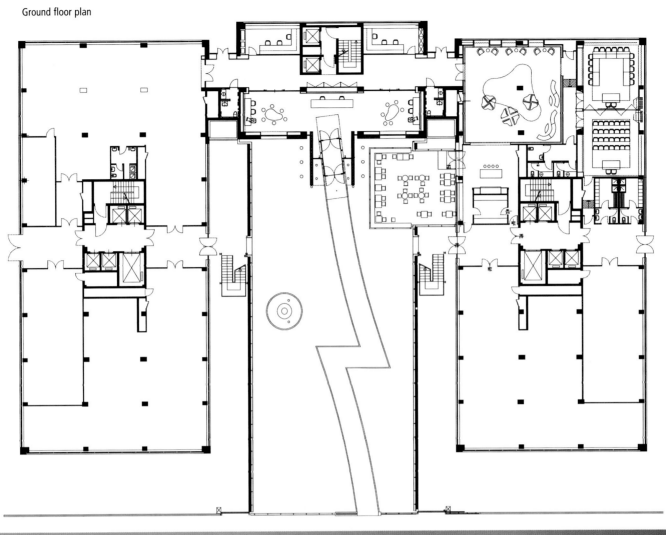

On either side of the entrance hall are two small glass-partitioned waiting rooms equipped with Internet access points and furnished with Moroso 'Saruyama' sofas and Kartell 'Moorea' chairs. An acid-green coloured wall hides the photocopier area as well as the elevators.

Hemmi-Fayet Architekten
Helbling Technik Offices]
Aarau, Switzerland

The project presented by the architects is based on the creation of two new areas: a spacious office area and a cafeteria.

In the first case, the rehabilitation of the building's original structure generated a large workspace. Some areas were acoustically protected with glass walls, and cloth panels were also used to isolate while allowing a sweeping view of the floor. Taking into account the engineers' wishes, these brightly colored panels both separate the different rooms and confer a characteristic atmosphere. The colors are inspired by the simulation models made by Helbling, a company that specializes in computing systems, air and space navigation simulation, as well as the mechanical and air traffic industry.

The cafeteria, as the second space intervened, presents an autonomous area within the existing shell. The irregular shape of the floor is ignored by the conceptual consideration of its axial structure, which is interrupted capriciously by a spiral staircase. They have also created a structure that includes a bench and ceiling suspended over the tables. These are covered with a red linoleum that is precisely molded to the existing structure, giving the sensation that the structure would go on indefinitely if it were not for the kitchen wall that abruptly interrupts the shiny stretch of red.

Finally, this space is flanked by two wide windows on one wall and a glazed corridor opposite. On the third side a spiral staircase goes up a sloping wall and the fourth side gives onto the sky blue kitchen.

Photographs: Hannes Henz

The personalized treatment and search for a particular identity for the two proposed areas did not pose any difficulty for the architects. For example, the engineers' opinion was taken into account as regards the brightly colored panels in the work area; colors were inspired by the company's simulation models. The cafeteria, in red and sky blue, seeks to create a comfortable rest area.

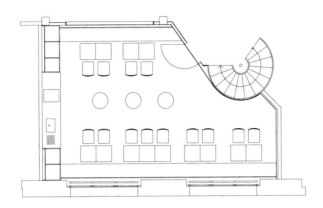

Cafeteria floor plan

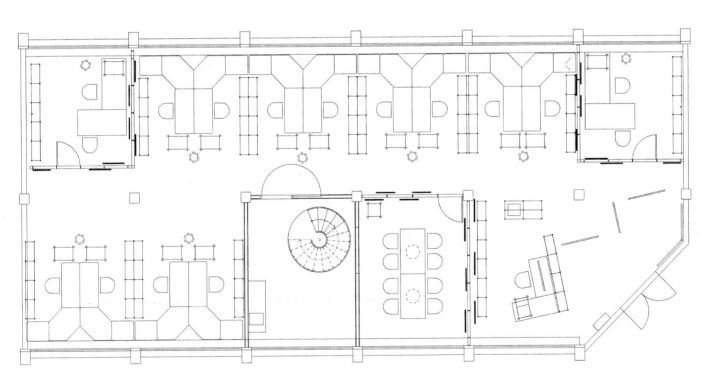

Offices floor plan

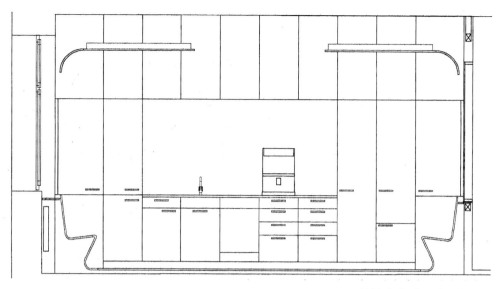

Cafeteria furniture elevation